HOW TO KEEP
YOUR FAITH IN AN
UPSIDE-DOWN WORLD

HOW TO KEEP
YOUR FAITH IN AN
UPSIDE-DOWN WORLD

Sarah Bowling

DESTINY IMAGE® PUBLISHERS, INC.

P.O. Box 310, Shippensburg, PA 17257-0310

"Speaking to the Purposes of God for this Generation and for the Generations to Come."

This book and all other Destiny Image, Revival Press, Mercy Place, Fresh Bread, Destiny Image Fiction, and Treasure House books are available at Christian bookstores and distributors worldwide.

For a U.S. bookstore nearest you, call **1-800-722-6774.**

For more information on foreign distributors, call **717-532-3040.**

Reach us on the Internet: **www.destinyimage.com.**

ISBN 10: 0-7684-2663-4

ISBN 13: 978-0-7684-2663-2

For Worldwide Distribution, Printed in the U.S.A.

1 2 3 4 5 6 7 8 9 10 11 / 12 11 10 09 08

ENDORSEMENTS

My dear friend Sarah will continue to inspire you through this book on *revolution* and living an upside-down life! Her encouragement will lift you and cause you to dream again, and open your eyes to practical wisdom on living an authentic life that pleases Jesus. Be blessed as you read.

—Darlene Zschech
Singer, Songwriter
Hillsong Church, Sydney, Australia

In this book, the author captures the essential nature of spiritual and social revolution and provides the wisdom from the past to help us in the 21st century understand the process for effective and positive change in our contemporary world. I highly recommend this work.

—Dr. Myles Munroe
Founder, Bahamas Faith Ministries International
Nassau, Bahamas

Sarah Bowling is just the person to write this amazing and revolutionary book. She is a personal friend, mighty woman of God, a true radical for Jesus, leading a fresh charge of zeal and passion from the Holy Spirit for such a time as this. We live in a time where the youth are interested in "extreme sports." Jesus is the ultimate of extreme and revolution with His extreme love and extreme sacrifice and commitment. Jesus asked "all." In this book she captures the true life of Jesus, mixed with the passion of the early followers of Jesus and a look through history. She brings all to the present day and gives the prophetic call for action now. Whatever your age, read this book at your own risk. You may never be "normal" again. Glory!

—Arthur Blessitt
Denver, Colorado

In every generation there are voices that call us to greatness. Sarah Bowling's new book, *How to Keep Your Faith in an Upside-Down World*, has given her a voice that challenges this generation to be everything we dream and dare to be so that we too will be a force that turns our world *upside down*! With historical to present-day insights, this book is a must for all who desire greatness in God!

—Gary Oliver
Pastor, Tabernacle of Praise
Fort Worth, Texas

Sarah has written a great inspirational book. Her insight on making dissatisfaction work for positive ends is remarkable. I believe this book will ignite revolutionary desires in your life to be a change agent for good. This book should be required reading in schools, colleges, universities, and businesses.

—John McMartin
Senior Minister, Liverpool Christian Life Centre
Sydney, Australia

Living in a part of Germany that has been under socialist reign and was freed not many years ago, I know what revolution can bring without any weapons but with prayer, which really produced that peaceful revolution (or change) in Germany in 1989.

This book has the potential to stir up and provoke some readers for the means that it is written: revolution. Some will be disturbed, some will stop reading because it questions our well-established status quo, but others will be challenged not to stop before reaching the goals they dreamed of all their lives. It's a dangerous book—you could end up where you always wanted to be but never allowed yourself to start the journey. Ready? Read it!

—Frank Heinrich
Captain, Salvation Army
Chemnitz, Germany

Sarah Bowling is a woman who is living a radical, passionate Christianity that is making a difference all across the world. *How to Keep Your Faith in an Upside-Down World* will stir, challenge, and inspire you to rise up and be all that God has called you to be—to do all that He has called you to do. Sarah has a great ability to unravel truth and inspire change. I strongly recommend this book.

—Christine Cain
Director, Equip and Empower Ministries
Baulkham Hills, Australia

Sarah Bowling hits you smack in the heart, and challenges you to get up and do something significant with your life. This book is written intelligently and passionately, and it will make you *think* about what you are doing with your life now and in the future. Life is too short to waste. *How to Keep Your Faith in an Upside-Down World* will help you evaluate what you need to do to become a true spiritual revolutionary for your generation.

—Rick Renner
Founder, Rick Renner Ministries

Sarah Bowling is a blessing to the Body of Christ. I believe with her that if we as Christians will totally surrender our will and submit to God, He will use us all to turn the world upside down for His glory. Reading this book will inspire you to live a life devoted to Jesus so that He can work through you to do the impossible. Blessings!

—CeCe Winans
International Recording Artist

I have known Sarah Bowling for the past 20 years. She is a great minister of the Word with a dynamic voice to this generation. In these volatile times, our culture is a noisy cacophony of uncertain voices. Sarah Bowling is a clear and powerful voice that is actively bringing transformation to a generation desperately in need of clear direction. She has been a consistent leader and is an incredible pastor with a heart for people and a savvy for effective ministry. Sarah has vibrant energy which captivates this generation and rallies them to a common goal. Her relevance and magnetism, along with her deep knowledge of the Word, create revival wherever she ministers.

—Jude Fouquier, Pastor
The City Church
Seattle, Washington

CONTENTS

FOREWORD

Are you ready to live the revolutionary kind of life—a life that impacts and inspires others? A life that meets pressing needs? A life that reaches desperate people with the love, power, and Word of God?

The book you are holding will capture your attention—and turn you into a "revolutionary" for God. As you read about the lives of individuals powerfully used to transform their world, you will discover the characteristics that made them world-changers. You'll also learn how to overcome discouraging thoughts and attitudes that can hinder you from taking action and becoming the world-changer God wants you to be.

Three years ago, my daughter, Sarah, had an experience that turned her world "upside down." She was a wife, the mother of three small children, pastor of a church, and my co-laborer in the ministry. She already had an abiding sense of purpose and a lot on her plate when she had a divine interruption—a point where God grabbed hold of her and set her heart aflame with an increased passion for souls.

Following this encounter with God, Sarah founded the humanitarian organization known as worldchild, which is dedicated to bringing

God's love, power, and Word to today's world. Additionally, God ignited within Sarah a passion to reach today's youth with the gospel, and with good reason: only 4 percent of Americans between the ages of 12 and 25 believe in God.

Many of today's youth have not even been inside a church or heard about having a personal relationship with God. In Sarah's words: "This generation is truly an 'unreached people group.' If they do not hear the message of Jesus Christ, we could witness the spiritual genocide of an entire generation!"

As you read this book, ask God for a clearer vision of your path. Wait on Him, and He will show you how you can make an eternal difference. It's time for you to turn the world *upside down* for God!

—Marilyn Hickey
Founder, Marilyn Hickey Ministries
Englewood, Colorado

INTRODUCTION

I've traveled a lot in my life—in more than 50 countries—and I've seen some quite amazing things. I remember visiting Lebanon when I was five years old and watching men walk around with guns and sit in sandbagged turrets with massive machine guns. As a preteen, I remember as we drove from Israel to Jordan, hearing bombs and artillery shelling in the background, which was a very scary experience.

When I was 19, I felt the ground violently shake under me as giant tanks rolled off of train platforms to "protect" West Germany in the Cold War. I was also 19 when I visited the Holocaust Concentration Camp of Auschwitz—a totally astounding experience that still leaves me speechless. I've also visited Cambodia where the Khmer Rouge executed between 15-30 percent of Cambodia's population in less than five years. Human history is full of atrocities and revolutions that went sour.

I believe that revolution directed by God doesn't have to be such a ruinous human endeavor. I also believe that God wants to interrupt the tragedy of human history on an individual level with a revolution based on His design. When God spoke to me to write this book, I was really excited. As I began to write, honestly, I became discouraged and gave up for awhile. God drilled me on this book last year and let me know that my quitting was actually disobedience in His eyes. Disobedience is an adjective I never want God to use when He is talking to or about me, so I got back on the horse and finished this book. My prayer for you as you read is twofold:

Number One: I pray that you will finish this book—read it in its entirety.

Number Two: I pray that God will transform you—that the book is not merely entertaining, but that the content is truly revolutionary for you.

Thanks for your time.

Enjoy the revolution God has for you!

Chapter 1

REVOLUTION IN PERSON

We live in a crazy and upside-down world. Bad is good, sick is excellent, the bomb is something terrific, and the list goes on. The heroes in our world include hip hop artists who kill and do drugs, professional athletes who often unapologetically lack standards, politicians who pretend to lead but more often look where the crowd is going and jump in front, and so on.

We live in an upside-down world, and I would venture to say that many of us haven't thought about how upside down our world really is. It's kind of like boiling a frog to death. If you put a frog in boiling water, he will jump out. But if you put a frog in room temperature water and slowly turn up the heat, eventually the frog will boil to death because he has become so accustomed to the gradual change in water temperature. Our world has become upside down slowly over time and incrementally through the lives of the masses. Specifically, our world has been revolutionized, turned upside down, by a few key lives over the past five or six decades. Let's consider a few revolutionaries:

A "Kroc" Revolution

Consider Ray Kroc. Ray bought the rights to a small hamburger restaurant in California in the mid-1950s. He had a vision to spread the "gospel" of hamburgers into multiple locations. From the result of his efforts, we now live in a world where food franchises are almost more common than privately owned restaurants. Ray Kroc started this revolution, and it has spread throughout the world. I've had McDonald's hamburgers on every inhabited continent, and experts tell us there are more than 30,000 McDonald's on the planet that serve 50 million people in 119 countries every day.[1]

A Mousey Revolution

Another modern revolutionary is Walt Disney. He was one of five children and mostly grew up in Missouri. Early on, Walt was very interested in art, and to make extra money, he would sell drawings to neighbors. In 1918, he joined the Red Cross and was sent to France, where he spent a year chauffeuring Red Cross officials and driving an ambulance, which he covered with Disney cartoons. After he returned to the U.S., he took on various jobs and was fired one time by a newspaper editor for a lack of ideas. Eventually, Walt headed to Hollywood and began writing and drawing more seriously, where he soon became a recognized Hollywood figure.

In 1937, during the peak of the Great Depression in the U.S., Walt introduced to the public the first full-length animated musical feature, *Snow White and the Seven Dwarfs*. The film cost almost 1.5 million dollars to produce, and to this day it is considered a monumental achievement in the motion picture industry. Walt Disney Studios continued to produce full-length animated classics such as *Pinocchio,*

Fantasia, Dumbo, and *Bambi.* Later, Walt dreamed of an amusement park, which opened in California in 1955. To this day, Walt Disney is a legend, and his Mickey Mouse is known around the world. Walt Disney revolutionized the world of entertainment with a mouse.[2]

Geeks Take Over the World

Another great example of a revolutionary is Bill Gates. He was born in 1955 and grew up in Seattle in a "normal" family. In junior and senior high school, he become very interested in computers and began programming when he was just 13 years old. He later attended Harvard and continued to work with computers. When he was a junior at Harvard, he dropped out and gave his energies and attention to a company he had just begun, Microsoft. Bill Gates believed that computers were going to be an integral part of the future in both a business and personal context. He saw them becoming usable by the masses— hence the personal computer. Because of this firm conviction, he and his team began developing software and applications to facilitate the common person's ability to connect to and benefit from computers.

Now, personal computers (PC) are an essential part of our daily lives. Most of us use e-mail for our communication. We can do our tax returns by computer. We use them to complete our school work and to create spreadsheets for our businesses. We use graphics and video editing programs, do research on the internet, and depend on databases to keep our personal records. Undoubtedly, computers are a vital component to our productivity. Whether you use an Apple or a PC, there is no denying the incredible impact these machines have made on our world within the last 20 years, all due to a few people with vision and passion. Bill Gates is one of those people.[3]

"Tanking" a Revolution

In a political context, let's consider the "Chinese Tank Guy." In 1989, there was an extremely large demonstration in Tiananmen Square in Beijing, China. Thousands of university students protested against government corruption and demanded greater political and social freedoms throughout China. This demonstration was not limited to Beijing. Many cities throughout China were experiencing the same upheaval and demonstrations. The government was tolerant of these demonstrations for some weeks, but as they began to increase in size and number, officials became increasingly nervous and uneasy about the public displays of insurgence. As a result, they called in the military to disband the demonstrations in Tiananmen Square. Tanks began to roll in, along with thousands of soldiers—armed not with anti-demonstration gear like tear gas or shields—but with weapons of war.

I'll never forget the cover of *Time Magazine*, which showed a picture of a lone man in a white shirt, carrying his briefcase, standing in front of a huge tank and holding up his hand in a gesture, asking the tank to stop moving forward.[4] He positioned himself in front of the tank so that it would have to roll over him to move forward. Like many of the demonstrators, he was telling the Chinese government's People's Army, "We are the people." To this date, no one is certain who the "tank man" was. He is an unknown person who stood up to make a difference, and his image still makes a powerful statement decades after this event. A small, unknown man held on to his convictions at great personal risk.

A Revolution of Care

One of the most powerful modern revolutionaries was Mother Teresa. She was born in Albania in a devout Catholic family that had deep, personal convictions about helping the poor and less fortunate. These convictions had a great impact on Mother Teresa's worldview. By the time she was 12, she decided that she was going to devote her life to helping the poor. She became a nun and moved to India to teach in a school. When she was about 35 years old, she received a call from God to "serve Him among the poorest of the poor."[5] From there, she moved to the slums of Calcutta to set up her first school, where she began ministering to the poorest of the poor.

In 1979, when she accepted the Nobel Peace Prize, she said her mission was "to care for the hungry, the naked, the homeless, the crippled, the blind, the lepers, all those people who feel unwanted, unloved, uncared for throughout society, people that have become a burden to the society and are shunned by everyone."[6] Throughout all of the ceremony related to receiving the Nobel Peace Prize, she stayed in her one dollar *sari* dress, and she convinced a committee that tried to honor her with a dinner to cancel it and use the money to feed 400 poor children in India for a year. She continued to expand her ministry to the poor in Calcutta and throughout India by opening homes for the dying, orphanages, and leper colonies. From there, with the Pope's blessing, Mother Teresa expanded her ministry to reach around the world. An example of her convictions was easily seen in 1982, at the peak of the Beirut siege. She persuaded the fighting groups to stop long enough for her to rescue 37 sick children who were stuck in a building between the fighting parties. Mother Teresa was a revolutionary. She lived by her convictions and turned as much of the world upside down as she could with her sincere care and authentic love.[7]

Improbable but Shocking

Here's an achievement that would seem improbable. Tom Dempsy was born without toes on his right foot. His family was always very encouraging and supportive, so he focused on his capabilities rather than his limitations. Eventually, he became a place kicker in the NFL (National Football League), and while playing for the New Orleans Saints, he kicked one of the longest field goals in NFL history—63 yards! He did this with a kicking foot that was half the size of his other foot.[8]

Conquer a Mountain and Start a Revolution

In 1952, Edmund Hillary attempted to climb Mount Everest, the highest mountain in the world. He failed on his first attempt, and shortly after that failure, he spoke to a group in England. A picture of Mount Everest hung in the room, and during his speech, Edmund shook his fist at the picture and said, "Mount Everest, you beat me the first time, but I'll beat you the next time because you've grown all you are going to grow, but I am still growing!"[9]

One year later, Hillary succeeded in becoming the first man to climb Mount Everest. Since Hillary's success, more than 2,500 people have successfully conquered Everest and the remains of about 200 who died in their attempt are still on the mountain.[10] Hillary started a revolution, and others have scaled his accomplishment due to his courage!

A Revolutionary Marathon

Men are not the only revolutionaries. Kathrine Switzer was a woman with revolution on her mind. Read what *Runner's World* said about Kathrine as one of the 40 most influential runners in the last 40 years:

> When Boston Marathon official Jock Semple hopped off a press truck four miles into the 1967 Boston Marathon and yelled "get out of my race" as he tried to rip the #261 off of K.V. Switzer, pictures of the altercation ran in newspapers around the world, changing women's running forever.[11]

"K.V." was 20-year-old Kathrine Switzer, the first woman to officially—if illegally—enter the Boston Marathon. "I knew that women were capable of running marathons if they were only given the opportunity," she said. Switzer's Boston finish created that opportunity. She went on to win the 1974 New York City Marathon, and was influential in the creation of the first Avon International Marathon in Atlanta in 1978, which featured 20 of the world's top female distance runners. She was also a prime lobbyist for the 1984 women's Olympic Marathon, and became an award-winning commentator at the Olympics and major marathons.[12] Kathrine revolutionized long-distance running for women.

A Race Revolution

What about discrimination? Righting injustices often requires a revolution. Nelson Mandela is an extremely powerful revolutionary. Nelson is a black man born in South Africa in the early 1900s under the apartheid regime, a government that racially segregated its population economically, socially, educationally, and by human rights, favoring the white "Afrikaaners."

Educated as a lawyer, he fought against the racial political system of government in South Africa until he was finally caught and imprisoned for 27 years for his "subversive" activity. He made the following statement during one of his many trials before the apartheid courts:

> I have fought against white domination, and I have fought against black domination. I have cherished the ideal of a democratic and free society in which all persons live together in harmony and with equal opportunities. It is an ideal which I hope to live for and to achieve. But if needs be, it is an ideal for which I am prepared to die.[13]

During his time of imprisonment, he became a worldwide icon for equality and freedom. In 1990, he was released from prison, and in 1993, he won the Nobel Peace Prize for his cooperative and constructive efforts to dismantle the apartheid system in South Africa. Nelson was and still is a revolutionary who turned his country upside down.

A Revolutionary at Heart

Let's finish our revolution adventure with a man who was himself thoroughly revolutionized! Saint Francis of Assisi was born in 1182 in Italy, the son of a wealthy merchant. His birth name was Giovanni—Italian for John—after the apostle John, and his mother gave him this name in hopes that her son would be a great leader in the Church. When his father learned of this name, he immediately changed it to Francesco since his father wanted him to be a merchant like himself.

Francesco was very well educated for his time, and he also enjoyed partying. By his own estimation, he was quite shallow and partied a lot. However, soon after a serious illness, he became more serious and began experiencing God, who confronted his superficial life. Through these experiences, he was challenged to become thoroughly devoted to his heavenly Father by renouncing the values of wealth and the pursuit of temporal things that he had learned from his earthly father. He began to rebuild a broken-down church based on a vision that he received from Jesus. He later understood this vision to mean rebuilding Jesus' Church through connecting people to Jesus in authentic simplicity. He devoted himself to a life of poverty, serving those who would receive his message of a loving relationship with Christ and turning his back on a comfortable, but common, life.

Saint Francis provided an interesting contrast to many of the Roman Catholic leaders of his day (Cardinals, Bishops, etc.) who were very wealthy men and lived rather extravagant lives. When Francesco took his vow of poverty to renounce the wealth of the world, he took a significant deviation from the normal church leader's behavior and lifestyle. Simply put, Francesco went back to the fundamentals of his faith, and this was a revolutionary way to live in his world. St. Francis of Assisi was a historical revolutionary who echoed into the future to speak to us today. There are millions of Franciscans throughout the world devoted to helping the underprivileged, connecting people to Jesus and bringing His love to all that God has created.

Revolutionary You

These are short, but compelling, biographies of people who revolutionized their world. There was nothing profound about their genetic makeup or upbringing that would create a chasm between their achievements and your potential. You have the potential to turn your world upside down, as well.

If Jesus is an integral part of your life and He is the Lord of your life, you can surpass Ray Kroc, Walt Disney, Bill Gates, and the

Chinese tank guy. You can become the revolutionary God designed you to be. Some of these people had a very committed relationship with Jesus, and some had none at all. Consider the ones who based their lives on the values of Jesus Christ—the revolutions they started continue today and they invite you to join their ranks. Looking at the others who did not have a vibrant relationship with Jesus, imagine, if they achieved what they did without Jesus, what Jesus can do with you. You'll notice that I didn't reverse that and say, "what you can do with Jesus." That would be an insult to the Author of the universe to think that He's going to take His marching orders from you. The most effective revolutionary is a person wholly surrendered to Jesus and committed to living out His will minute-by-minute and day-by-day.

As you continue to read, you will learn about a man in the Bible named Paul who gives us a great example of how to live for someone who is worth dying for—Jesus Christ. Maybe you're reading this, and you don't have Jesus as part of your life, and you're not convinced that you need Him. I'm not going to try to talk you into having Jesus become part of your life, but I would ask that you keep reading because you'll find some incredible principles that, when consistently applied, will make you more effective than you have ever been. If you do have a relationship with Jesus, then you'll be really excited to know that He is very eager to ignite a revolution in you to turn your world upside down. Continue with me to see Jesus' blueprint for revolution through Paul's life.

I'm so excited you're taking this adventure!

Chapter 2

REVOLUTION IN THE BIBLE

Everyone has heroes—some good and some bad, but we all have heroes. In the first chapter, we looked at some modern-day heroes. Heroes give us inspiration, they fuel us, and we reference them in our minds when thinking of decisions, possibilities, and direction in our lives. All of us have thought, *what would* _____ *do in this situation?* Or *I wonder what* _____ *would think about this?* One of my heroes in the Bible is Paul. To me, he's an incredible giant—he lived with tremendous passion, focus, conviction, drive, and purpose. While he was as much human as I am, I find myself thinking about him when I get in tough situations, when I need to make a difficult decision, or when I'm struggling in living my convictions.

He is very inspiring to me. In fact, people who lived in his time were deeply moved by Paul in both positive and negative ways. There were people who had never met Paul who were extremely concerned about him. He rapidly developed a reputation for being a very persuasive person.

Thessalonica

For some people, Paul's abilities were very threatening. For example, in the city of Thessalonica, a group of men got pretty wound up about Paul's arrival in their city. Thessalonica was a very significant city in Paul's time. Some historians say that it was the most populated city on the Macedonian province. Whatever its population, it was located in a very strategic position along the *Via Egnatia* (a road that led through Thessalonica to Rome), and it was also a port city that was easily accessible for trading purposes with modern Turkey.[1]

Paul probably understood that Thessalonica was extremely important if he wanted to spread the good news of Jesus throughout Macedonia. So he went to this city and immediately began to speak to the Jews in the synagogue. Many of his listeners, as well as many Greeks and prominent women, were deeply moved and became Christians. Many of those who heard Paul's message but did not become Christians, became extremely hostile toward Paul and his message to the point of forming a mob and starting a riot (see Acts 17:1-9). Sometimes revolutionaries begin miniature revolutions that they never intended to ignite!

The leaders of the riot stormed the house where Paul was staying, looking for him. Instead of finding Paul, they grabbed the owner of the house, Jason, and drug him to the city leaders, where they said, "These men who have turned the world upside down are now among us!"

In today's world, these might have been some business or civic leaders, men and women of influence in your city, who would go to the mayor, city council, or other significant officials. These people who opposed Paul left their jobs and families to confront the city leaders. Think what the newspapers, journalists, television reporters, and general media would have to say if Bono, Bill Gates, or Nelson Mandela were to show up "to set up camp" in your neighborhood. We would naturally expect such individuals to turn our neighborhoods upside down—because of who they are and what they have accomplished in their lives.

Lystra

In Thessalonica, the men who were concerned about Paul and Silas coming to their city had good reason to be uptight. Perhaps they had heard about Paul and Barnabas' experience in Lystra (see Acts 14:8-18). Through them, God had healed a crippled man. Now it was wonderful that this crippled man was healed, but there was a legend in this area about two Greek gods, Zeus and Hermes, coming to visit this region. The legend said that only one couple graciously received these Greek gods. Because of the poor reception by the inhabitants, Zeus and Hermes became angry and supposedly destroyed the area's population in a flood. Now, when the people of Lystra saw this amazing miracle of the lame man being healed, they decided that the same mistake with Zeus and Hermes wouldn't be repeated.[2] As a result, a large number of the people came out of the city gates to meet Paul and Barnabas, and they brought sacrifices to them to worship them as gods for the display of "their" power in healing the crippled man.

After Paul and Barnabas tried to clear up the confusion as to whose power brought the healing to the crippled man, some Jews from Antioch came to Lystra to stir up trouble against Paul and Barnabas (see Acts 14:19-20). So in a very short amount of time, the crowd did a total about-face. The same crowd that wanted to offer Paul and Barnabas sacrifices of worship, was now transformed into a mob that stoned Paul and left him to die. The believers of Lystra gathered around Paul, prayed for him, and he got up and went *back* into the city. The next day, Paul and Barnabas set out for the nearby city of Derbe. But Lystra had been turned upside down by Paul's message and the power of God. Out of Paul's ministry in Lystra came his letter to the Galatians, Christians from the Roman province of Galatia, the province where Lystra was located.

Ephesus

In many cities, after Paul's visit to Thessalonica, he saw virtual revolutions! For example, Ephesus was a city devoted to idol worship, economic prosperity, and hedonism. It was the capital for the worship of the Greek goddess Artemis, also known as Diana to the Romans. The worship of Diana was a powerful religious and economic force in Ephesus. Legend said that a wooden image of Diana fell from the sky and landed right near Ephesus. Consequently, Ephesus became the capital for Diana worship, the so-called goddess of life, and the official Diana Temple was built in Ephesus. Since Diana worshipers were not always able to get to the Temple, many different kinds of small idols and statues were made to assist in worshiping the goddess. Additionally, Diana worship included the practices of ceremonial prostitution and sacrifices. The idol worship created a very lucrative business built around making idols of Diana.[3]

Not only was Ephesus known as the center for Diana worship, it was also renowned for its rampant prostitution and its occult practices. When Paul started out ministering in Ephesus, there were 12 believers who joined him. He worked there for almost two years, and at the end of two years, some historians estimate that up to *half* of this city was converted to Christianity.[4] Ephesus was revolutionized socially, religiously, economically, and even politically. Jesus accomplished some very dramatic miracles through Paul's ministry in Ephesus, and the city burned their occult relics and lost a significant portion of the revenue stream that accompanied the Diana idol-making industry. There was such a dramatic change in the city of Ephesus that a riot ensued, and the mayor had to settle everyone down so they didn't attract the attention of the Roman authorities (see Acts 19). Now *that's* upside down.

Athens

Furthermore, Paul went to the geographical heart of Greek philosophy, Athens, and confronted the philosophies and religions of the day. Athens had been a springboard for many great thinkers, including Plato, Socrates, Aristotle, Pericles, and others. Note that Socrates is often credited for creating the foundation for Western philosophies. Great ideas, philosophies, religions, and men were all discussed and debated in this city throughout many centuries. Even after the Roman Empire was established and the heyday of Greek philosophers had waned, Athens was considered the university city for the Roman Empire. So when Paul came to Athens, it had an established culture of debating ideas, an interest in new philosophies, and an openness to thoughts and religions. In a modern context, this city would be known for its ideological tolerance. Clearly, Athens was a city recognized for its intelligentsia, but it was also a city full of idol worshipers. So when Paul visited Athens, he saw statues of many gods. In fact, Athens was so full of idols in Paul's day that Petronius, a writer in Nero's court, said, "Our region is so full of deities that you may more frequently meet a god than a man."[5] These idols undoubtedly included statues to Roman and Greek gods, along with many others.

Paul began his discussion in Acts 17:22-23 by saying,

Men of Athens! I see that in every way you are very religious. For as I walked around and looked carefully at your objects of worship, I even found an altar with this inscription: TO AN UNKNOWN GOD. Now what you worship as something unknown I am going to proclaim to you.

Paul went to the very heart of Greek philosophy to bring a revolution—to turn the world upside down. From this brief introduction, a number of people from the city at the heart of Western philosophy believed what Paul said and became followers of Jesus (see Acts 17:34).

Paul and His Companions

So who were these men, Paul, Silas, Barnabas, Timothy, and others who traveled with Paul? What were they like? Did they have lots of money, lots of education, or political influence? What did they have that made such a dramatic impact on the cities they visited? What did they do to impact history with such significance? Were they just historical aberrations? To begin, these men had virtually no money, they traveled extensively, and they generally supported themselves by their own means. They worked hard and endured all kinds of opposition, conflicts, hardship, imprisonments, cruel prejudices, and traumas— even to the point of facing death. Paul said in Second Corinthians 11:24-28:

Five times I received from the Jews the forty lashes minus one. Three times I was beaten with rods, once I was stoned, three times I was shipwrecked, I spent a night and a day in the open sea, I have been constantly on the move. I have been in danger from

rivers, in danger from bandits, in danger from my own country-
men, in danger from Gentiles; in danger in the city, in danger in
the country, in danger at sea; and in danger from false brothers.
I have labored and toiled and have often gone without sleep; I
have known hunger and thirst and have often gone without food;
I have been cold and naked. Besides everything else, I face daily
the pressure of my concern for all the churches.

Yet these men, particularly Paul, turned the world upside down.

Here's something to think about: in many respects, before Paul became the revolutionary, Christianity was still in its beginning stages with (as a generous guess) no more than 25,000 followers. Paul was able to reach no fewer than 2 million people with the good news of Jesus Christ, the Messiah and Savior of the world. He was martyred in about A.D. 65. By A.D. 100, Christians were about .013 percent of the Roman Empire population (which equals approximately 7,500 believers). In another 100 years (A.D. 200), the number of Christians had grown to .36 percent of the Roman Empire. By A.D. 300, Christians made up about 10.5 percent of the Roman Empire.[6]

I would call this revolutionary growth, especially considering the amount of persecution Christians endured, the fact that they were ostracized from communities, and the internal struggle that the Church faced as it sought to clarify what was to be considered standard and accepted orthodox doctrine. Paul and many other men and women were tremendously used by God in both their lives and their deaths to spearhead the revolution of Christianity that has continued for almost two millennia.

When we look specifically at Paul, he was instrumental in spreading this revolution by writing letters that were carried by friends to different groups of people. These men and women spread this revolution by simply living out the reality of Jesus in their lives, by talking with people, traveling, and giving their lives to a cause greater than themselves. They spread this revolution without the internet, television, radio, cell phones, text messaging, mp3 players, computers, books, printing presses, or any such modern communication tools. There were no means of mass transit; most people moved from point A to point B by walking or maybe by riding on a donkey or horse. How on earth did these men, under such horrific conditions, with such primitive methods, turn the world upside down? Moreover, how does this relate to you?

What About You?

If we were to be thoroughly transparent, I think almost all of us have fantasized about doing incredible things. When I was little, I dreamed about being an astronaut and landing on the moon. As I got older, I fantasized about being a great basketball player (a very grandiose illusion). And I would venture to say that even as you read this, you can think of some really incredible things that you have dreamed of doing—being a professional athlete, becoming a billionaire, inventing some major technology to transform humanity, or something else. I believe that almost all of us have had daydreams of doing something truly incredible and changing the world. Of course some of our daydreams can be nonsense, but I also have this echo of truth that rattles in my heart that says we were each created with the potential to turn our world upside down.

Do you hear that echo in your heart? Do you still dream "what if"? Nothing revolutionary happens if you don't dream, if you don't explore in your heart, if you don't imagine, "what if." I believe with everything inside me, that each of us has been given the breath of the Almighty God to live extraordinary lives beyond our natural potential. The people you read about in Chapter 1 had, and some still do have, big dreams. In fact, the Bill and Melinda Gates Foundation has donated more than $1.5 billion to global health initiatives since 2003 (including the elimination of polio and improving vaccine availability, among other things).[7] While you may disagree with some of the other programs that the Bill and Melinda Gates Foundation supports, it's difficult to argue with some of their goals.

Have you ever dreamed about eliminating HIV? Have you ever dreamed about sharing Jesus with your school? Have you ever dreamed about being a missionary for Jesus? Have you ever dreamed about getting rid of some of the evil in our world? Revolutionaries are dreamers—nothing great happens without a dream, without someone being unsatisfied with the status quo.

In being dissatisfied with the status quo, we must also be careful, because we've seen examples in recent history of individuals who fantasized about doing revolutionary things in a negative way. Some people dream about violence and destruction—and of these dreams, nothing good ever comes. Think about Dylan Klebold and Eric Harris. These two young men forever changed the way we view school safety due to the Columbine High School massacre they orchestrated. On April 20, 1999, these two high school seniors realized their fantasies of mass destruction by killing 12 classmates, one teacher, and themselves after setting bombs and traps throughout the school. They fantasized for at least a year about death, destruction, and hurting people. They were revolutionaries in a negative way, and they reached into the future and influenced others to do even more gruesome things than they did. Consider Seung-Hui Cho, the South Korean who killed more than 30 students, including himself, on April 16, 2007, at

Virginia Tech University. Cho looked up to Harris and Klebold and considered them to be martyrs. Cho, Klebold, Harris, and others initiated negative revolutions from their negative fantasies. These are three sad endings of men who had tremendous potential but were very sick.

Let's open our eyes and see the need for a positive revolution in the communities in which we live, work, go to school, and play. So what about the world you live in? What about your neighborhood, family, school, and workplace? Let's consider our own potential and the world in which we live. If these three men could have such a negative impact, what kind of positive impact can we have in our world with the power of Jesus?

Think back to Paul; he went far beyond his natural potential. If you read about his background, he was trained to be a leader in Judaism with lots of schooling and leadership development. He also had the genetic pedigree to be a person of great importance in Judaism. When he came to Jesus, however, he was changed and consequently revolutionized the world in which he lived. How did he live such a fantastic life? How did he turn the world upside down almost every place he went? And more importantly, are there things that we can learn from Paul and apply in our lives to help us uncover our divine potential to live extraordinary lives filled with passion, focus, conviction, drive, and purpose?

If you want to watch someone who had such passion, focus, conviction, drive, and purpose, consider watching the movie, *Amazing Grace*. This movie, set in the late 1700s and early 1800s, is about William Wilberforce, a very strong and determined revolutionary figure. Wilberforce was a political leader in England who held extremely deep convictions about the need to stop the perpetuation of slavery.

At that time, England was a leading world power, and slavery was the accepted norm in the economic world. Wilberforce, however, was strongly opposed to slavery, fundamentally, on the grounds of its moral poverty. He felt that it was essentially anti-human to "own" another person and control their life. Wilberforce spent two decades fighting slavery in the British government as a member of Parliament. After many setbacks, the efforts of Wilberforce and many of his friends were finally rewarded with the passage of the Slave Trade Act in 1807, which abolished slavery in the British Empire, thus ending nearly 300 years of legalized slavery. Wilberforce was a revolutionary. He turned his world upside down and made his life count for something more than his own survival and existence.

Here are some thoughts to consider about *revolution*:

John F. Kennedy said, "Those who make peaceful revolution impossible will make violent revolution inevitable."[8]

Fidel Castro said, "A revolution is not a bed of roses. A revolution is a struggle between the future and the past."[9]

Ernesto Che Guevara said, "At the risk of seeming ridiculous, let me say that the true revolutionary is guided by a great feeling of love. It is impossible to think of a genuine revolutionary lacking this quality."[10]

Eric Hoffer said, "We used to think that revolutions are the cause of change. Actually it is the other way around: change prepares the ground for revolution."[11]

The Excuse Evasion

This section of the book reflects on a reason that you or someone else might be considering to validate disengaging from something God may be asking from you. Whatever the evasion, we have all had these excuses from time to time.

I'm not smart enough. The truth is that there's not a single person on the planet who hasn't had this thought from time to time. Some of us have this very thought running through our mind and think that we have ample reason to justify our thinking. For example, my husband is a very smart man—he knows a lot about a lot of things. If I'm not careful, I can feel that I'm not smart when I'm around him because of my ignorance in different areas about which he is knowledgeable. But consider the flip side; just because you are very smart doesn't mean that you're going to accomplish what God has for you. And just because you're ultra brainy doesn't mean that you're guaranteed to be the revolutionary that God is having you think or read about in this book. Here are some great quotes from nay-sayers of recent technology that illustrate this point:

Thomas Watson, chairman of IBM, said in 1943, "I think there is a world market for maybe five computers."

A Western Union internal memo from 1876 read, "This 'telephone' has too many shortcomings to be seriously considered as a means of communication. The device is inherently of no value to us."

In response to Fred Smith's paper proposing a reliable overnight delivery service, a Yale University management professor wrote, "The concept is interesting and well-formed, but in order to earn better than a 'C,' the idea must be feasible." Smith went on to found Federal Express Corp.

Harry M. Warner, of Warner Brothers, said about the new "talking pictures" in 1927, "Who the hell wants to hear actors talk?"

In 1962, in response to the Beatles, Decca Recording Company said, "We don't like their sound, and guitar music is on the way out."

Steve Jobs, founder of Apple Computer, Inc., recounts his attempts to interest Atari and Hewlett-Packard in the work that he and Steve Wozniak had done on their newest idea, the personal computer:

> So we went to Atari and said, "Hey, we've got this amazing thing, even built with some of your parts, and what do you think about funding us? Or we'll give it to you. We just want to do it. Pay our salary, we'll come work for you." And they said, "No." So then we went to Hewlett-Packard, and they said, "Hey, we don't need you. You haven't got through college yet."

In 1929, just months before the American stock market crash that initiated the Great Depression, Irving Fisher, a professor of economics at Yale University, said, "Stocks have reached what looks like a permanently high plateau."

Lord Kelvin, President of the Royal Society and name-sake of the kelvin scale, said in 1893, "X-rays will prove to be a hoax."

Bill Gates, now worth billions of dollars, said in 1981, "640K ought to be enough for anybody."

And in response to Thomas Edison's electric light bulb, the British Parliamentary committee described it as "Unworthy of the attention of practical and scientific men."[12]

To sum it all up, if you could do something significant and not fail, what would you do? What is something that concerns you—that gnaws at the back of your head—that you would change if you could? Read on to begin *your* revolution!

Chapter 3

REVOLUTION FOR BEGINNERS

ignite: from the Latin word *ignitus*;
"to cause to burn or set fire to"[1]

In 1789, the French Revolution ignited for a variety of reasons—poor economic management, famine, absolutism in the French government, the culmination of a change in thinking through Enlightenment ideas, as well as many other contributing factors. Revolutions happen in lots of different ways—political, economic, social, information, technology, etc. Earlier, we read about some different kinds of revolutions—a food industry revolution instigated by Ray Kroc, the entertainment industry revolution led (in part) by Walt Disney, the computer revolution significantly impacted by the leadership of Bill Gates, and many others.

Revolutions are caused by a variety of factors. But it's an absolute truth that nothing changes without the germination of an idea. Nothing changes without a dissatisfaction with the status quo, and nothing changes without a commitment to change—without a commitment to a cause.

Cause and Effect

Revolutions exist because of a cause, and the world holds no shortage of causes. If you watch around you, you'll notice many causes that people want you to join—the cause of saving endangered species of animals, the cause of mothers uniting against drunk drivers, the cause of global child immunizations, the cause of stamping out poverty and starvation. The list of equally noble causes continues.

As we look at causes around the world, it is wisdom to consider the endurance factor of these causes. The endurance factor asks: *If this cause were to be completely realized, how eternal are its results? How lasting are the consequences of this cause? Will they echo into eternity?* Many wars have been fought, and many noble things have been done, but unless you're a history junkie like me, such things can get lost in the passage of time.

Think back to some of our revolutionaries and their causes in Chapter 1—Bill Gates with computers, Ray Kroc and hamburgers, Edmond Hillary climbing Mount Everest, and the others. These men and women accomplished significant things and changed their worlds.

But revolutions and causes come and go. Everything in our lives is in a state of flux—is constantly changing. In the Bible, Solomon, the wisest man who ever lived before Jesus, accomplished incredible feats. He led his country into massive economic improvement, built some of the most magnificent structures of his time, and developed a political organizational structure for his reign that was tremendously admired as the epicenter for wisdom by kings and leaders throughout the world. Yet in spite of all of his achievements, he called them "meaningless" no fewer than 35 times in the Book of Ecclesiastes.

If you're like me, you want to give yourself to something of meaning with eternal value—something that will outlast your 70 years or so on this earth. Of all the men and women we talked about in Chapter 1, only the revolutions of three of them will echo into eternity.

Mother Teresa, Nelson Mandela, and St. Francis of Assisi ignited revolutions that have eternal implications. These individuals joined themselves to something larger than their limited lives on this earth. They were absolutely human and had many of the same human failings that we all experience. The eternal difference of their lives, however, is found in what they gave their lives to.

The Cause of Christ

I want you to consider the cause of Jesus Christ. Many of us who have Jesus as an integral part of our lives are delighted to understand that God has a wonderful afterlife waiting for us. Furthermore, many of us have experienced His wonderful presence throughout our lives and appreciate His daily involvement. But Jesus did not humble Himself by taking on a human form, confront the sin of humanity, and experience His brutal crucifixion and glorious resurrection just so that we could revel only in the victory He purchased. His death, resurrection, and ascension did not happen only to improve your life or to secure your eternity. If this were true, then shortly after we gave our lives to Christ, we should have arranged for our funerals so that we could live in eternity with Jesus, the author of our life.

Jesus did everything that He did, and went to the effort of recording His teachings in the Gospels, with the intention of helping us live revolutionary lives on earth. Consider what Paul said in Philippians 2:13, "For it is God who works in you to will and to act according to his good purpose." He intends to use those who believe in Him to reach and transform the world in which we live. He intends to increase His Lordship on the earth by using us as revolutionaries—to turn the world upside down.

The cause of Christ is not only to bless our lives through His love, but I believe, the cause of Christ is more importantly to transform us and our communities through the love and power of Jesus. He wants to use us to accomplish Philippians 2:10-11: "That at the name of Jesus every knee should bow, of those in heaven, and of those on earth, and of those under the earth, and that every tongue should confess that Jesus Christ is Lord, to the glory of God the Father." Our cause is to allow Jesus' Lordship—through us—to turn the world upside down, one life at a time.

Let me tell you about the father of one of my friends. We'll call this friend's dad "Bob" for anonymity purposes. Bob grew up in a Christian home, and he had some really tough sexual problems. Even before he was a teenager, he was obsessively interested in sex, and by the time he reached his teen years, Bob was really knowledgeable and experienced with sex—it had become more than a hobby. As Bob aged, he considered himself to be a good Christian for the most part. He thought that getting married would help address his sex drive, but he found that marriage wasn't enough. He tried to stay faithful to his wife, who became pregnant, but he wasn't able to manage this obsession. In fact, he had become a sex addict, even though he was a regular church attendee and a leader in Bible studies and small groups.

Bob lived a double life as a secret sex addict and as a "strong" Christian husband and father for more than 20 years—until one day he was arrested for soliciting a prostitute. It was at this point that Bob was confronted with the realities of his life. When his wife was about ready to take their children and leave him, he turned to God, as well as some support groups and therapy, to conquer the addiction that was ruining his life.

Through many years, conversations, confrontations with truth, and primarily God's grace, Bob is a recovered sex addict and now leads a ministry to help set others free from all kinds of addictions and habits. He has been revolutionized and is allowing the change that Jesus started in him to filter through his life, reaching others with the transforming truth and power of Jesus. Bob found the cause of Christ to be effective enough to change his life. He discovered a cause that is worthy enough to enable him let go of destructive behaviors in exchange for the liberating truth that He has found in Jesus. Bob is a modern-day revolutionary.

Authentic Living

Not only is the Christian revolution alive today, but it has been growing since Jesus came to the earth. Think about when Christianity was in its infancy stages before a.d. 300 and it was illegal to be a Christian. At various times, Roman emperors and various political and social leaders would go on a rampage and kill Christians and Christian leaders. One of the greatest Christian leaders, Polycarp, was a pillar in the Christian Church in the second century. The people and political leaders in the area where Polycarp lived wanted to silence Christianity, so they joined together to martyr him. The crowd came out to the farm where Polycarp was living, and he welcomed them with water and food to eat. He knew that they had come to kill him, but he asked for an hour to pray before they took him.

When he went with the crowd, they dragged him to the arena of his city and tied him to a stake. Usually, martyrs beg for mercy and leniency. Polycarp wasn't a "normal" martyr. The proconsul overseeing Polycarp actually pleaded with him to renounce Jesus so that he would not be burned at the stake. Polycarp replied, "Eighty and six years have I served Him, and he never did me any injury; how then can I blaspheme my King and my Savior."[2] Throughout the centuries and throughout the world, you will always find examples of individuals who would rather die than deny their faith in Jesus.

Living for Christ with such conviction helps clarify the difference between pursuit of personal gain and authentic Christianity. There have always been people who have claimed to be Christians for the primary purpose of advancing their personal agendas. These individuals have misused, misdirected, and distorted the cause of Christ to promote their own ideas and selves. Unfortunately, this is not an uncommon occurrence. Human tendency is to try to shape the world to revolve around us. The Jesus revolution changes us to shape our lives around Jesus—nothing more and nothing less. To join the eternal revolution that Jesus initiated 2,000 years ago, we must consider the changes He makes within our hearts.

A great modern-day example of an individual who allowed Jesus to change his heart is Dietrich Bonhoeffer. Bonhoeffer was a German theologian born in the early 1900s who was opposed to the Nazi regime in its entirety. Bonhoeffer felt that the Nazi Christian justification for killing Jews was completely false, and he openly fought against the Nazi propaganda. He was extremely passionate about his beliefs to the point of creating secret seminaries in Germany to train Christians in biblical Christianity and to counteract the subversive doctrine the Nazi system was propagating. On several occasions, Bonhoeffer was confronted and arrested for his anti-Nazi position, and it began to be very dangerous for him to continue to live in Germany. An American theologian arranged for Bonhoeffer to come to America right before World War II, primarily to escape prison and possible death and to also tour around America giving theological lectures.

Upon arriving in America, Bonhoeffer changed his mind, and within a month he was back in Germany. He wrote to his American friend who had made the arrangements for him to tour in America,

> I have made a mistake in coming to America. I must live through this difficult period of our national history with the Christian people of Germany. I will have no right to participate in the reconstruction of Christian life in Germany after the war if I do not share the trials of this time with my people.[3]

Upon his return to Germany, Bonhoeffer was soon imprisoned and ultimately killed, with Hitler's direct knowledge, for standing up for his beliefs. Dietrich Bonhoeffer is a modern martyr—he found that the cause of Christianity was worth giving his life for. Knowing that he would soon be killed, he wrote in a farewell letter, "This is the end for me—the beginning of life."[4]

Paul in the Bible had a similar view of life. At the end of his life, some of his finishing words were:

> *For I am already being poured out like a drink offering, and the time has come for my departure. I have fought the good fight, I have finished the race, I have kept the faith. Now there is in store for me the crown of righteousness, which the Lord, the righteous Judge, will award to me on that day—and not only to me, but also to all who have longed for his appearing* (2 Timothy 4:6-8).

Men like Paul and Dietrich Bonhoeffer were revolutionaries within the eternal context. Their lives echo words of truth to us today and into eternity. Their lives counted for something beyond themselves.

The Excuse Evasion

I'm married, so I'm exempt from doing anything radical. In actual truth, being married in our world is quite radical. What's even more radical is to *stay* married. We'll talk statistics later, but here's something interesting that my husband and I believe about marriage—we believe that marriage was designed by God to help you fulfill God's purpose together in a greater way than you could as a single person. Case in point—Abraham needed Sarah to be the father of nations that God had called him to be (see Gen. 17). And Mary needed Joseph and his dreams to keep Jesus from being killed by Herod (see Matt. 2:13).

In a similar way, my husband, Reece, helps me fulfill God's purposes for my life, as I do the same for him. Not only do God's purposes for our lives include raising godly children, but Reece is a pastor and I'm a Bible teacher. While we're both very different and have different giftings, such diversity is essentially a tremendous strength to our marriage. Reece is very analytical, smart, and takes the time to process information. On the flip side, I'm not nearly as smart as he is and I tend to be more impulsive and risky. We balance each other well—so he doesn't get stuck in a quagmire of analysis and so I don't jump off the deep end without having first put some thought into my actions. I also try to encourage him in his pastoring, parenting, and as his counterpart. He supports me in lots of ways. At present, he stays home with the kids on Tuesday nights so I can study biblical Greek at the seminary in town. We both work to support each others' calls and not just our own.

Many other examples also show that marriage can be a powerful asset in God's hands which helps us grow into the people God has designed us to be. Maybe one of your challenges is that you're married to someone who isn't as strong of a believer as you are. The revolution God has for you, in part, is to be an authentic follower of Christ in your home around the person who probably knows you better than anyone else. Truthfully, I want to be the most Christ-like with the people who I love the most, my family.

Here's some food for thought:

George Bernard Shaw wrote, in his 1903 essay, "Maxims for Revolutionists," which serves as an addendum for his play, *Man and Superman,* "Beware of the man whose God is in the skies."[5] While George Bernard Shaw was clearly anti-religious and had some very controversial ideas, he nevertheless by his warning, communicates that there's something of substance to those who have religious underpinnings—an assertion that Christians should consider from an avowed mystical humanist.

Anthony J. D'Angelo, in his book of wisdom from his college years, *The College Blue Book,* wrote, "Promise yourself to live your life as a revolution and not just a process of evolution."[6]

Jesus said to His disciples,

If anyone would come after me, he must deny himself and take up his cross and follow me. For whoever wants to save his life will lose it, but whoever loses his life for me will find it. What good will it be for a man if he gains the whole world, yet forfeits his soul? Or what can a man give in exchange for his soul (Matthew 16:24-26).

The 12 apostles took His words to heart. *Fox's Book of Martyrs* lists their causes of death as follows:

1. Andrew—crucified.

2. Bartholomew—beaten, then crucified.

3. James, son of Alphaeus—stoned to death.

4. James, son of Zebedee—beheaded.

5. John—exiled for his faith; died of old age.

6. Judas (not Iscariot)—stoned to death.

7. Matthew—speared to death.

8. Peter—crucified upside down.

9. Philip—crucified.

10. Simon—crucified.

11. Thomas—speared to death.

12. Matthias—stoned to death.[7]

As Tertullian, the early church leader and apologist, wrote, "The blood of the martyrs is the seed of the church."[8]

Chapter 4

LESSON 1

concern—from the Latin word *concernere*;
com- "with" + *cernere-* "to sift";
"to mix with; to be interested, engaged"[1]

confront—from Latin or Middle French word con-
fronter; *com-* "with" + *frontem-* "forehead";
"to face in defiance or hostility"[2]

There are many powerful illustrations of revolutions that turned the world upside down. One example relates to the Viet Minh efforts to remove the French from Vietnam in the first half of the 20th century. The French had superior military equipment compared to the Viet Minh. The French also had many other resources that the Viet Minh lacked. Because of their perceived superiority, the French decided to set up a military base far removed from their supply lines and home base. This base was located in North Vietnam in a place called Dien Bien Phu. Here, they created a "viable" military base, complete with an airstrip to create a supply line to their resources.

Even though Dien Bien Phu was surrounded by hills, the French were not concerned about any vulnerability because they felt that the hills or mountains were steep and high enough to create a sort of "defense perimeter." The Viet Minh saw the hills as a great opportunity and staging ground for artillery bombardment of the French. The Viet Minh acknowledged that the mountains were indeed steep and high. Their solution, however, was to disassemble their artillery equipment at the bottom of the hills, carry the pieces up the mountains, and reassemble them at the top of the mountains—ready for an artillery barrage that thoroughly took the French by surprise!

The Viet Minh bombarded the French with artillery for many days and continued their assault by creating a strangle hold of trenches around the French base, until after several months, the French surrendered. The leader for the Viet Minh forces who defeated the French at Dien Bien Phu was a man named Vo Nguyen Giap. Giap was raised in a small village in Vietnam by parents who owned and worked their own land. He grew to be a revolutionary who wanted to see the Japanese, French, and later the Americans leave his country. He was deeply motivated for his country to be able to rule itself, and he joined the Viet Minh in the 1940s. Simply put, he was concerned about Vietnam and his concern translated into both small and large actions. A son of a peasant farmer turned his world upside down by defeating a world power based upon his concern for his country.[3]

Revolutionary Self-Transformation

So how can we turn our world upside down? Let's go back to Paul as our example of a revolutionary. How did Paul and his friends come to be known as "these who turned the world upside down are now among us" (Acts 17:6)? Paul was an interesting fellow. He was a zealous person before He gave His life to Jesus. He did things with all of His heart. His life turning-point happened when Jesus confronted Him on the road to Damascus (see Acts 9). By looking at this confrontation with Jesus, we can evaluate and apply the steps that Paul went through in his transformation, even if we don't consider ourselves to be as zealous as Paul.

Paul went from being a person completely opposed to Jesus, to being a person completely devoted to Him. Paul went from persecuting the followers of Jesus to promoting them. He changed from a person who didn't comprehend the cause of Christ to a person who argued for and clarified the cause of Christ.

So how did this transformation happen? I believe that the answer to this question is also the answer to your transformation. You may be reading this, thinking, *I can't turn my world upside down. I've got too many personal problems.* Or you may think, *Let someone else change the world—I've got enough on my plate right now.* Or you may think, *I can't turn the world upside down—I'm inadequate or incapable.* Maybe you're a *reluctant revolutionary.*

To give you some encouragement, let's remember the Viet Minh. In the early to mid-1900s, thousands of men and women were involved in the Viet Minh effort to throw the French out of Vietnam. I believe that many, if not all, of the Viet Minh associated with the victory at

Dien Bien Phu had similar reservations—and yet they were all transformed for a cause.

How can you be like that? The answer to this question rests in the change that impacted Paul on the road to Damascus. Simply put, Paul underwent five steps in his transformation.

Concerned for the Cause

The first step in Paul's transformation was that he was *concerned* for the cause. In Acts 9:1-2 we read:

Meanwhile, Saul [Paul] was still breathing out murderous threats against the Lord's disciples. He went to the high priest and asked him for letters to the synagogues in Damascus, so that if he found any there who belonged to the Way, whether men or women, he might take them as prisoners to Jerusalem.

Saul (Paul) didn't like Christianity and wanted to eradicate it; in a backward way, he was very concerned about the cause of Christianity. Similarly, we need to be concerned about the cause of Christ and the world in which we live. Let's consider our world:

Mental Health

In America, an estimated 22.1 percent of Americans ages 18 and older—about one in five adults—suffer from a diagnosable mental disorder in a given year. In 2000, suicide was the third leading cause of death among 15- to 24-year-olds. Approximately 18.8 million

American adults, or about 9.5 percent of the U.S. population ages 18 and older in a given year, have a depressive disorder.

Approximately 19.1 million American adults ages 18 to 54, or about 13.3 percent of people in this age group in a given year, have an anxiety disorder. Anxiety disorders include panic disorder, obsessive-compulsive disorder, post-traumatic stress disorder, generalized anxiety disorder, and phobias (social phobia, agoraphobia, and specific phobia). Anxiety disorders include panic disorder, obsessive-compulsive disorder, post-traumatic stress disorder, generalized anxiety disorder, and phobias (social phobia, agoraphobia, and specific phobia). Community surveys have estimated that between 2 percent and 5 percent of Americans experience binge-eating disorder in a six-month period.[4]

Drug Usage

What about drug usage among our youth—the future of America. In a survey conducted in 2004, more than 70 percent of high school seniors had been drinking within the last year.[5] Maybe drinking isn't that big of a deal for you, but what about illegal drugs? More than eight percent of high school seniors have used cocaine at some point.[6] In 2003, 29 percent of all students in grades 9 through 12 reported that someone had offered, sold, or given them an illegal drug on school property. More than 34 percent had used marijuana in the same period.[7]

Family Life

Living with a person of the opposite sex before marriage is rapidly becoming the normal experience and marriage is increasingly becoming old fashioned. Between 40 and 50 percent of all marriages will end in divorce.[8] And at least half of the children under 13 years of age live in a blended family situation.[9]

Sexuality

We continue to have an increase in sexual activity among our youth, and some surveys have concluded that 70 percent of high school seniors have been or are sexually active. This, of course, increases the transmission of sexually transmitted diseases.[10]

Entertainment

Our entertainment industry continues to desensitize the American population to violence, crude behavior, and sexual content and orientation. While I agree that our society will always have liberal and conservative elements with varying degrees of influence, my question is, at what point do individuals stop listening, watching, and being indifferent and start engaging with their world?

Religion

Finally, experts tell us that one-third of "baby boomers" (people between the approximate ages of 40-60 years old) have Judeo-Christian values and consider themselves Christian. In contrast, 4 percent of the people under the age of 25 years consider themselves to be Christian.[11] This is a very drastic decline and predicts an extremely different moral terrain for the future than what has been the accepted norm of the past.

Generation X

Let's look at the first generation to be dramatically influenced by these statistics. Consider Generation X. It was during the formative years of this generation when prayer and the Ten Commandments were taken out of public schools. This was the generation that marked the turning point in "mass divorce." This generation experienced the "latch key" syndrome (both parents working when kids came home from school on a regular basis). The sexual values of this generation were shaped by the sexual revolution in the 1960s and '70s.

This was the generation that was being born at the time of Roe v. Wade (the legalization of abortion), and they're numerically the smallest generation that lives in America today.[12] This generation was the first generation in America to be raised without any significant Judeo-Christian underpinnings. So is it any surprise that the generation to follow the Gen-Xers has very few Judeo-Christian values or even interests? If you'd like to add more fuel to the fire, consider the common belief among this generation that most Christians are merely hypocrites. It is a normally accepted perspective that Christians are generally more "talk than walk"—the antithesis of a revolutionary!

Chances are, you may be one of these statistics. Please don't take this information as a condemnation of what has happened to you or of the choices that you may have made. Rather, I bring out this information to raise awareness and to possibly stir up some past pain or hurt in your heart that would ignite concern for the people around you. I believe that these trends and numbers need to concern you because each number potentially represents the family living next to you, the man who rides the elevator with you at work, the people in the apartment next to yours, the woman on the treadmill at the gym, the person who bags your groceries at the grocery store, the guy on your basketball team, or the girl in your class.

Confronted by the Cause

To turn our world upside down, we have to first of all be concerned about the cause of Christ! I believe that many of us *are* concerned, and I think that is noble. However, only being concerned will not render a change. Truthfully, I'm concerned about lots of things—I'm concerned about the possibilities of the greenhouse effect on our atmosphere. I'm concerned about the AIDs rate in Africa. I'm concerned about the prevalence of sex in the media, and about child prostitution in Asia. I'm very concerned about a lot of things! However, if we are only *concerned*, we join the billions of people throughout the world who are worried about various people, things, and causes, but never do anything. Since God wants to use us to turn the world upside down, we cannot be merely concerned. We need to take the next step—to be *confronted* by the cause.

Paul was dramatically confronted by the cause of Christ on the road to Damascus. In Acts 9:3-5, we read:

> *As he [Paul] neared Damascus on his journey, suddenly a light from heaven flashed around him. He fell to the ground and heard a voice say to him, "Saul, Saul, why do you persecute me?" "Who are you, Lord?" Saul asked. "I am Jesus, whom you are persecuting," he replied.*

Paul had a face to face confrontation with Christ. Paul was literally knocked to the ground in his confrontation with Jesus—Paul was turned upside down. If we are going to turn our world upside down, we must first be turned upside down ourselves. We cannot do what we have not experienced.

Consider your life as it relates to being confronted by Christ. Ask yourself these questions: Has your life been turned upside down by Jesus? Have the values in your life been radically changed by a confrontation with Jesus? Have you become stagnant in Jesus' confrontation in your life? If you have been turned upside down by Jesus, how has His confrontation affected your life? Paul's world was radically changed when Christ *confronted* him on the road to Damascus. Has your world been radically changed?

When I consider this question, it makes me think about a time in my life where my world was turned upside down by Jesus. Right before I was married, I had a very radical experience with Jesus. I was raised as a pastor's kid in a very strong Christian home. My parents modeled their Christianity for me, and I had my own comfortable relationship with Jesus. I wasn't necessarily turning the world upside down for Him, but I valued His leadership in my life. I was also very intellectual and unemotional. I wasn't comfortable with strongly emotional expressions of Christianity, and was much happier with a conservative and intellectual approach to and display of Christianity.

The week before I was married, I had a radical, life-changing experience with Jesus. I attended some revival meetings at a different church. In these meetings, I had a carpet experience where I fell on my face and experienced Jesus confronting me about my life. He spoke to me clearly and said that He had a different plan for my life than the one I was pursuing. Before this experience, my plans for after I got married were to go to graduate school and get my doctorate to teach at a university level. I relished the intellectual environment, and felt that I could thrive quite well there. Nevertheless, when Jesus confronted me, He let me know that my plans were not aligning with His plans and that if I honestly said that He was my Lord, then I would need to surrender to His plans.

I remember lying on the floor, sensing God's presence all over me, and saying "yes" to His plans, "yes" to His agenda, and turning my back on the things that I had planned. When I told my fiancé about this experience, he wasn't initially very thrilled about this change. We nevertheless got married, and to make the long story short, we are both fully engaged in spreading the revolution of Jesus throughout the world, including our immediate communities.

This carpet experience transformed me. Before this experience, I wanted virtually nothing to do with ministering to other people and was very comfortable pursuing a higher education and an intellectual approach to life. After this confrontation, I was incredibly impassioned to reach out and make God's Word real and relevant to people. My world was completely revolutionized, and I have subsequently gained a significantly deeper understanding of what it means to surrender to Jesus' lordship. When you are turned upside down by Jesus, your life, with its decisions, values, and judgments no longer rests in your hands. The control of your life belongs to another—it belongs to Jesus.

When we talk about giving Jesus control of our lives, sometimes in Christian contexts the phrase becomes cliché—almost overused. It can become easy to say that Jesus has authority over our lives when we don't really mean it. Let's face it, in many of our major decisions, we sometimes get God's input, but that's exactly how we see it—as His input and not His authority. Sometimes it's easy to fall into perceiving God as another one of our friends with some really good advice rather than seeing Him as the final authority in our lives. Maybe we just want to see Him as a good friend because, ultimately, we don't want His control over us. Whatever the case, we will never turn our world upside down until *we* have been turned upside down—until Jesus is literally the final decision maker in our lives and not just a person with good advice.

This is true because the environment in which we live fosters independence, indulgence, and tolerance. As long as we go along with our environment, we'll never make a radical impact on it. And I sincerely believe with everything in me that God does not intend for us to live non-impacting lives. I believe that "We were meant to live for so much more, / Have we lost ourselves?"[13]

Once again, I ask you to consider these questions: Has your life been turned upside down by Jesus? Have the values in your life been radically changed by a confrontation with Jesus? Have you become stagnant in Jesus' confrontation in your life? If you have been turned upside down by Jesus, how has His confrontation affected you? After considering all of these questions and reflections, maybe it's time to make a fresh surrender to Jesus' lordship.

Excuse Evasion

I'm scared. Fear can be completely debilitating. I remember a time in my early 20s when I was so afraid, I made some extremely bad decisions. But because of fear, I couldn't see how bad those decisions were. Thankfully, my dad confronted me and asked me why I was making such bad choices. I began to cry, not to be manipulative, but because I was sincerely choked up about what I perceived to be happening in my life at the time. Because my dad had really great insight, after listening to me cry for a little bit, he said, "Sarah, the reason you're making these bad choices is because you're afraid. Listen to me—if you run from fear now, it will chase you for the rest of your life!" This one phrase changed me and helps me to this day to not allow fear to control me. Don't be like the farmer in the following story:

> There was a farmer sitting on his front porch when a friend popped in for a visit. "How's your wheat going this year?" asked the visitor.
>
> "Ain't got any," replied the farmer. "I didn't plant any because I'm afraid the weevil will get into it and ruin me."
>
> "Oh, well how's your corn?"
>
> "Ain't got any," replied the farmer. "I didn't plant any because I'm afraid the crows will eat it all up and ruin me."
>
> "Oh, well how are your potatoes going?"
>
> "Ain't got any," replied the farmer. "I didn't plant any because I'm afraid the tater bugs will poison them and ruin me."
>
> "Well, what did you plant this year?" asked the confused visitor.
>
> "Nuthin," replied the farmer. "I just played it safe."[14]

Chapter 5

LESSON 2

compelled: from the Old French word *compellir*; "to drive together"; from com- "together" + *pellere-* "to drive"; "to force or make happen"[1]

corrupted: from the Latin word *corruptus*; "to destroy, spoil, bribe," *rup-* pp. stem of *rumpere-* "to break"; "to taint, destroy"[2]

I n the 1700s, the world was changing quite dramatically. Many inventors were excited about the possibilities of improving the lifestyles of the average person. Some of their inventions included the steam engine, the fly shuttle, the spinning jenny, and power loom, all of which greatly affected the making of textiles.

Simply put, men saw an opportunity, using the industrial advances of their day, to make mass production improvements to the clothing that was commonly worn. Men such as James Watt, John Kay, James Hargreave, and Edmund Cartwright were not only concerned about the world around them, they were also compelled by the technological opportunities that were in front of them. As such, these men were instrumental in revolutionizing the textile industry, and today we daily wear the outcomes of their inventions.[3]

Compelled by the Cause

Here's an interesting parallel: Paul was a tentmaker. He didn't revolutionize the profession of tent-making, but he did change the communities that he worked in, and what he experienced through Jesus Christ continues to beckon us today. That experience began when Jesus confronted Paul on the road to Damascus. Regardless of how powerful this confrontation was, Paul had a choice. He didn't just lie on the ground and wallow in the confrontation. He took the next step. He got up, moved forward, and obeyed what he heard from God while he was on the ground. He was *compelled* by the cause of Jesus.

What does it mean to be compelled? *Compel* comes from the Latin roots *com,* meaning "with," and *pellere,* meaning "to drive." When we combine these words, we figure out that compel literally means "to drive with" or "to cause to act." Paul was not only concerned about the world in which he lived; he wasn't just confronted by the cause of Jesus on the road to Damascus; he was *compelled*—he acted on his concern.

In Acts 9:6, Jesus said to Paul, "Now get up and go into the city, and you will be told what you must do." It wasn't enough for Him to confront Paul and knock him to the ground. Jesus wanted to turn the world upside down through Paul—and He wants to turn your world upside down through you! So after confronting us, He tells us to get up, to get moving, to do something—to be compelled by the cause. It's not enough to be concerned about the world that we live in. It's not enough to have been confronted by Christ—to say that He is our final authority. Paul would have never turned the world upside down by reveling in the power of Jesus to knock him off of his feet. Jesus asks each of us to make a difference in our world by doing something—by being compelled by the cause.

Paul immediately acted on the confrontation that He received from Jesus. In Acts 9:8, it says, "[Paul] got up from the ground, but when he opened his eyes he could see nothing. So they led him by the hand into Damascus." Paul *acted* on his confrontation with Jesus. He got up and went. I have seen people who have had an amazing encounter with Jesus just sit in the same place and never go anywhere with that encounter. Once we have had an encounter, we must allow the momentum to continue in and through us; otherwise we can become stagnant and hypocritical Christians.

What *Compelled* Looks Like

So when we are compelled by the cause, what does that look like? *Compelled* means to act; when we are compelled by the cause, we act out our concern. Think about the lady who thought she saw a little girl in trouble in a convenience store. The lady didn't act on her observation immediately, but later she felt compelled to make sure that the little girl was safe. So she went back to the store and viewed the videos. She saved the little girl's life since she had been abducted by a sexual predator.

Or how about the young man who was staying with an older gentleman who was dying? A nurse in a hospital brought an anxious young man to an elderly man's bedside. She said to the older gentleman, "Your son is here." After she repeated herself several times, the gentleman opened his eyes. Because he was heavily sedated with pain medication, he couldn't see the young man standing next to his bedside very well. The elderly gentleman reached out his hand and the young man took it, squeezing it to let him know he was there. The young man stayed with the older gentleman, holding onto his hand and giving words of encouragement throughout the night. The dying man didn't say anything, but he held onto his son's hand until dawn when he died.

The young man placed the older man's hand on the bed and went to let the nurse know of the death. The nurse offered the son some consolation that she hoped would help him in his loss, but the young man interrupted her and asked, "Who was that man?" The surprised nurse said, "I thought he was your father." The young man replied that he had never seen the older gentleman in his life. The quizzical nurse asked why he stayed through the night with a dying man whom he did not know. The young man said, "I knew he needed his son, and his son just wasn't here. When I realized he was too sick to tell whether or not I was his son, I knew how much he needed me...."[4]

Engaging Our Worlds

Both of these examples show us in practical ways what it means to be compelled by the cause of Christ in our communities. We become engaged with advancing the cause of Christ in many ways, often different from the two examples you just read. We can get active in our church by serving in the youth ministry, by being a greeter at the doors, by opening our home to a small group, by participating on church missions trips, by giving our money, by joining a prayer group, and by not just sitting in the chair once a month and criticizing the sermon. We become engaged with advancing the cause of Christ by helping out at homeless shelters, by being a caring person in our classrooms, by being friendly and kind with our co-workers (and not just at Christmas), by shoveling our neighbor's sidewalk when it snows, by making a meal for the single mom who lives in the apartment next door.

These are just a few examples of what it looks like to be compelled by the cause—of creating opportunities to connect people to the love of Jesus in each of us. I believe with all of my heart that we can turn our worlds upside down through allowing the tangible love of Christ to be expressed through our practical lives on a daily basis. I also thoroughly believe that our communities will not change until we individually engage with the cause of Christ—until we become Jesus with skin and take Him into our world. The weight of turning our individual worlds upside down does not rest on our pastor or a televangelist or on our spouse or a great Bible teacher. The weight of turning our worlds upside down doesn't even rest on the likes of Bill Gates, Nelson Mandela, or anyone else, for that matter. The weight of turning our worlds upside down rests squarely on our shoulders because it is in our communities that God has placed us.

There was a theme in some of the *Star Trek* movies and *Next Generation* episodes related to the "Borg." The Borg were a species who had been assimilated into a collective, group-think type of society. Their primary objective was to conquer other species to assimilate them into their culture. When they confronted a non-assimilated species, they would say, "We will assimilate you. Resistance is futile." Now if you're much of a "trekkie," you know that the Borg were very disturbing because their assimilation efforts eliminated all individuality and because they were in many ways very violent in their efforts to conquer.

As Christians, Jesus commands us to spread the Gospel and to develop devoted followers of Christ, as He said in the Great

Commission in Matthew 28:19-20. In contrast to the Borg techniques, Christianity conquers through love—the love of Christ compels us. In Second Corinthians 5:14, Paul wrote, "For Christ's love compels us, because we are convinced that one died for all, and therefore all died." Let's not allow Jesus' efforts to compel us to dwindle into apathy and indifference toward the communities in which we live. Let's allow His fire in our hearts to grow until we can say, "I no longer live, but Christ lives in me" (Gal. 2:20) and because of who Jesus is in me, I'm alive and can make a difference in my world!

Corrupted by the Cause

After we begin engaging our worlds, what then? Where do we go from there? How do we transform our worlds? What did Paul do next? We read about Paul's next step in Acts 9:9: "For three days he was blind, and did not eat or drink anything." Then, in Acts 9:20-22:

> *At once he began to preach in the synagogues that Jesus is the Son of God. All those who heard him were astonished and asked, "Isn't he the man who raised havoc in Jerusalem among those who call on this name? And hasn't he come here to take them as prisoners to the chief priests? Yet Saul grew more and more powerful and baffled the Jews living in Damascus by proving that Jesus is the Christ.*

The fourth step that Paul went through was that he was *corrupted* by the cause.

You may ask, "What does it mean to be corrupted by the cause?" The cause of Christ changed him; it changed who he was. Let's think about corruption. If you have ever lived in a part of the U.S. that gets a lot of snow, you know that in the winter rock salt is spread on the roads to help the ice melt and to improve driving conditions. The salt often splashes up under the cars. Water and salt splashing onto the metal of the car frequently causes rust. Soon the rust starts to work through the metal of the car and it can eventually *corrupt* and corrode an entire car. In this example, there's a transformation process—a slow ruining.

It's the same way with Christianity. Christianity is meant to corrupt you. The cause of Christ begins to corrupt you so that you become ruined to the destructive things of the world and you feel increasingly alive when you live for Christ. Christianity should ruin for you those things that used to be integral parts of your life. When pornography used to be a big issue for you, now you're ruined to it because of the cause of Christ. You've been corrupted, and you've experienced a transformation.

Let me share a practical example from my life of how the cause of Christ corrupted me. As I mentioned earlier, during my mid-20s I had a really strong encounter with Jesus right before I was called into the ministry. This experience literally turned my world upside down. It was a confrontation. Before this confrontation, I wanted to be really smart. I was very dedicated to pursuing intellectual endeavors. Before my confrontation with Christ, I remember taking a class in readings in Russian History. In class, I read about Lenin's five-year economic plan. I remember that as I studied this plan and how it was developed and how it was implemented, I thought it was an incredibly cool thing to understand. I loved all of the scholarly historical debates, dialogue, thought processes, writing, and intellectual banter. While I still think it is great to be smart, something happened to me that changed me and corrupted an "idol" that had been a driving force in my life.

After I was confronted with the cause of Christ, Jesus started to corrupt me—I was turned upside down. Shortly after this confrontation, I continued to pursue my master's degree. When I started my master's in more earnest, I remember going to school and liking it more. What really captured my heart wasn't the scholarly dialogue, the pedantic banter, the research, or the writing—it was God's call on my life to teach the Bible and bring His love, power, and Word to today's world. I totally understand that God has called each of us to different careers, assignments, and seasons—bringing God's presence and truth into our daily living no matter if in the classroom, farm fields, or board room. For me during this season, it was captivating to think about the 20,000 students who were enrolled in school with me. I remember walking the hallways and sidewalks, passing by people, watching them in my classes, thinking about their lives and their eternities.

At lunchtime, I would hang out in the cafeteria during the most crowded times, and it would break my heart because I so desperately wanted to reach the people in the room for Jesus. I would sit next to different people and strike up conversations in hopes of opening a door to share about how wonderful Jesus could be in their lives. There were times when I would come home and cry because I didn't have an opportunity that day to share Jesus with someone. I had been corrupted. I still maintained good grades, but my focus and passion had shifted. The previous drive to learn and be smart had been corrupted. I had made education and intellectualism into a miniature god, an idol, so God corrupted my thinking so I could more completely love and serve Him.

One time, I intentionally took a class called the History of Mysticism. This class was packed with people who were all interested in spiritual things. In essence, the class was the history of the New Age religious movement. You may ask, "Why did you take that?" I took this class because I knew that the people in this class were hungry for something spiritual. I would sit in class and cry inside and ask God, "How can I reach them? What can I do?" My grade in the class was a very distant concern for me compared to the people who were in the class with me. This was a transformation for me. The content of my classes had now taken a back seat compared to the true value of the people contained in my classes. I wanted to reach the people in my classes, and I would ask God to use me to reach them. As opportunities were available, I would share my faith with the friends that I made in my classes.

Many times I would come home upset because I hadn't reached more people. Some days, Reece would come home from work to find me crying, and ask, "What's wrong with you?" Invariably, I would be upset because I didn't get to share Jesus with anyone that day. My husband didn't understand at this time why I was like this. But I was corrupted by the cause—I was ruined.

Have you been corrupted by the cause of Christ? You'll never turn your world upside down unless you start making progress on this path from being concerned to being confronted, from being confronted to being compelled, from being compelled to being corrupted.

Let's talk about the world we live in for a moment. My world is in Denver, Colorado, and the neighborhood where I live. My world is my workplace, the places where I work, the schools and activities that my kids are in. My world is the neighborhood in which I jog and ride my bike. It includes the television and Internet audience that God has given my mother and me. My world is my church. My world is the grocery store where I shop. My world includes the friends that I hang out with and allow into my life—and even more. That's my world.

What's your world, and who lives in it? No one else has access to your world like you. No one does the exact same things with the exact same people that you do. No one works with all of the people you work with, talks to your neighbors like you do, takes classes with the same friends, shops at your grocery store, hangs out with your sphere of friends, *and* works out in your gym. This is your world (more or less), and you have to turn your world upside down, one life at a time. So when you consider your world, you need to ask yourself if you are honestly concerned about the cause of Christ. Most of us are concerned about what is happening around us and to many of the people in our worlds. If not, maybe this is a good time to ask God to open your eyes to the people in your world.

Consider these questions for reflection. After being concerned, consider if you have moved to the next step of being confronted by the cause of Christ. Have you been flipped upside down? Does Jesus, your Lord, make the decisions in your life? Have you been compelled by the cause? Are you acting on your faith or has it become a social accessory? Are you interacting with life and people? Have you insulated yourself to the point of disconnecting from society? Have you been so corrupted by the cause that a transformation has occurred in you so that it's no longer you who lives, but Christ who lives in you? I pray that, as you read through this book, you will allow God to walk with you on this path—concerned, confronted, compelled, and corrupted—to the final destination: consumed.

Excuse Evasion

I'm too busy. Now here's the most classic and commonly used excuse that we all over-exercise. Truthfully, we often haul this one out when there's something that we don't really want to do, and we all seem to accept it as a "hall pass." Face it, we're all busy with the things that we want to do—watching television, going to movies, chilling at home, going for ice cream, hanging out with our friends. There's an endless list. But we all have the same quantity of time—24 hours each day—it's just a matter of how we use it.

Think about this: A study was conducted several years ago at Princeton University to figure out in what circumstances people would be "good," or at least helpful. In this study, two psychologists asked two groups of theology students to give a lecture of their choice on either the Good Samaritan or their motives for studying theology to a group of students in a building across campus. At the same time, the psychologists had chosen an actor to be on the path to the building, pretending to be sick by coughing and being slumped over. Before each lecturer from the first group set out for the building across campus, the psychologists told them they were late for their speaking appointment. The students in the second group, however, were led to believe that they had ample time.

So, what do you think the responses were? Who was most likely to help the ailing student? I would think that the individuals most likely to help the secret actor were the ones who had decided to lecture on the Good Samaritan. But, there was a big difference between the behaviors of the students. The difference wasn't, however, related to their lecture topic. The choice of their topic had no effect on their behavior. Generally, the same number of Good Samaritan speakers and theology motivation students stopped to help. The difference was in how much of a hurry the students thought they were in. Only 10 percent of those who thought they were running late stopped. In contrast, 60 percent of those who were told they had plenty of time stopped to help.[5]

Time can be deceptive—be careful not to get lured into the trap of excusing your life away into meaningless oblivion. As Eleanor H. Porter, author of the novel *Pollyanna,* said, "The influence of a beautiful, helpful, hopeful character is contagious and may revolutionize a whole town."[6] Or, as Jesus said:

> *But I tell you who hear me: Love your enemies, do good to those who hate you, bless those who curse you, pray for those who mistreat you. If someone strikes you on one cheek, turn to him the other also. If someone takes your cloak, do not stop him from taking your tunic. Give to everyone who asks you, and if anyone takes what belongs to you, do not demand it back* (Luke 6:27-30).

Chapter 6

LESSON 3

consume—from the Latin word *consumere*;
"to use up, eat, waste"[1]

Let's look at an interesting example of a man who was *consumed* with a cause. One of the primary leaders of the Russian Revolution in 1917 was Vladimir I. Lenin. Lenin's father worked for the Russian government but died of a cerebral hemorrhage when Lenin was 16 years of age. Then the next year, Lenin's oldest brother was hanged for participating in a plot to kill the tsar (Russian emperor), and his sister was banished from his family for being with the brother who was hanged.

These events were extremely pivotal in Lenin's life. He began to pursue political interests that were opposed to the tsar and his rule. Because of his interest in Marxism, he was arrested on more than one occasion and became a very devoted and intense revolutionist. He traveled extensively throughout Europe and wrote articles for many publications. One of his most famous and influential publications was a pamphlet he wrote called, *What is to be Done?* Lenin claimed that three out of five workers in Russia had read this pamphlet. He continued to write and travel during World War I and knew that he must return to Russia when the war was over. To help him sneak back into Russia, the Germans allowed Lenin to travel through Germany hidden on a train on its way to Russia in hopes that Lenin would destabilize an already fragile Russian government.

Consumed by a Cause

When he arrived in Russia in April, 1917, he became the leader of the Bolshevik movement and sought to overthrow the established government. Through a series of events, the Bolsheviks took charge of the Russian government, and Lenin became the first leader of the Soviet Union. He died in 1924 at the age of 53, consumed by the revolution to which he had devoted his life.[2]

Personally, I'm not a big Lenin fan. I admire his passion for the cause he devoted his life to, although I don't personally agree with his tactics nor values. Consequently, I don't think his motives were purely to help the working man or peasant in Russia. Nevertheless, he was instrumental in leading a communist revolution that continues to negatively impact the world today. He is an example of a man obsessed by a human revolution that affected humanity in a negative way. One disastrous effect was the starvation of millions of farmers due to the national Soviet campaign to take away private land ownership and create public collectives to cultivate crops and raise livestock. While this economic move may have seemed noble in principle, it was completely devastating in practice. Some historians estimate that up to 12 million people were killed as a result of this effort to de-privatize land ownership that continued into the 1930s.[3]

Additionally, the leadership of Lenin led to the rule of Joseph Stalin—one of modern history's most ruthless dictators. Historians tell us that Stalin was responsible for the deaths of no less than 4 million people, due simply to political reasons and personal paranoia.[4] Unfortunately, history is full of revolutions that have been completely disastrous to the human race. Is it possible for us to be consumed by a revolution that will create something different from the usual human results? Let's go back and look at Paul's experience as the example for the revolution that Jesus wants us to join—so that we can be part of something divine or "un-human."

The Jesus Revolution

Paul was *consumed* by the cause. After Paul's Damascus road experience, and after he was blind for a few days, God healed him and initiated him into the Body of believers. His testimony was so powerful that the Jews tried to kill him:

Now after many days were passed, the Jews plotted to kill him. But their plot became known to Saul. And they watched the gates day and night, to kill him. Then the disciples took him by the night and let him down through the wall in a large basket (Acts 9:23-25 NKJV).

When Paul found out that the Jews wanted to kill him because he gave his life to Jesus, he didn't change his mind, waffle, or second-guess his commitment. Paul was *concerned* about the cause of Christ and then he was *confronted* by Christ Himself. After being confronted, Paul was *compelled* to do something about it, and then the *cause* of

Christ began to *corrupt* him, making him un-useful to the previous values he had in his life. He took the next step from being *corrupted* by the *cause* of Christ to being *consumed* by His *cause*. Not only was he *changed*, but Jesus had *captured* his heart, and he was *consumed* with Christ!

Laying Down Our Lives

When Paul encountered this attack, he had received Jesus only a few days earlier. Within these few days, his life was already being threatened for the cause of Christ. At that point, many of us would say, "Well, this Christianity stuff has sure been interesting. But maybe I could kind of ease my way into this, so I don't get killed! Or maybe better yet, how about I just kind of ease my way *out* of this Christianity stuff and just say it was a phase." For most of us, being asked to lay down our lives for Christ only a few days after inviting Him into our lives would be over the top—that would be too much sacrifice. Even for those of us who have been Christians for years, I'm not very convinced that many of us would be willing to give our lives for the cause of Christ.

Maybe this goes to the heart of the weak state of the Christian walk with many today. Perhaps the world, neighborhood, or community where we live hasn't been changed for Jesus because we as individuals haven't been changed. Generally speaking, you do not do what has not been done to you. Consider your relationship with Jesus. Does it ignite your heart? Does it fuel your days? Does it guide your decisions? Does it energize the purposes in your life? Does it convict your wrong thinking or behaviors? Where is the passion? Where is the zeal? Have you ever been consumed with Jesus? Wherever you are in your walk with Jesus, either a newbie or a veteran, I pray that you will never lose your first love—that first fire that captivated you with Christ, that obsession that made the world vibrant with the life of Christ, that rest and assurance that you're completely accepted and loved by Him.

When you are consumed by something, it becomes the default to which your actions, thoughts, desires, and heart return to moment by moment, day by day, and year by year. Paul is a good example to look at for this default. He was consumed with Jesus! In essence, he said, "I have found something worth dying for!"

I remember an experience that I had the summer before I went into high school. My parents sent me to a Christian camp in Fort Scott, Kansas. I had an extremely powerful experience with God during those two weeks. When I came home, I was passionate to follow Jesus, to read my Bible, to know more of God, and share His love and truth with anyone who would listen. I remember later that summer, I would go into downtown Denver with a group from our church every Friday night to walk the streets and share Jesus with anyone who would listen. I became consumed by the cause of Christ, and this affected my every waking moment during that summer. In other words, I had found something worth dying for. Self-preservation is one of the most powerful forces in our lives. We will go to almost any length to preserve our lives. And yet there are a few things that we would be willing to sacrifice our lives for. Most parents would die for their children. Many of us would give our lives to save our family members. But for the most part, finding people willing to believe in a cause to the point of sacrificing their lives is a rare thing. And yet, when we do see this commitment to sacrifice, we also see that incredible things can happen.

A Man Consumed

In the mid-1800s, God raised up a British man by the name of Hudson Taylor to bring the Gospel to China, where millions of people had never heard the name of Jesus. Upon hearing about Jesus, a Chinese man asked Mr. Taylor, "Why did you not come sooner?" The middle-aged man was one of the leading officers of a sect of reformed Buddhists in China. He had long sought truth by studying Confucianism, Buddhism, and Taoism; but not until he heard the Gospel of Jesus did he find rest for his soul.[5]

This experience is an example of the extensive work that God accomplished through Hudson Taylor, who founded the China Inland Mission. Taylor was determined that every province in China would hear the Gospel. It seemed an impossible task because of the size of the country, the immense size of the population, and the closed political situation. But Taylor believed that the responsibility for the mission rested with God, not with men. He was consumed with his desire to reach China for Jesus.

When Taylor was 21 years old, he sailed for China and arrived in Shanghai, where he immediately began learning Chinese. At the time of his arrival, foreigners were extremely limited in their access to China—they could only visit five port cities. Nevertheless, Taylor burned with desire to reach the millions of Chinese who had never heard of Jesus. Taylor ignored the political restrictions and journeyed along the canals, spreading the good news of Jesus.

Eventually, Taylor had to return to England due to poor health. While there, he finished his medical studies. He also worked on a Chinese New Testament and organized the China Inland Mission organization. After a few years, he returned to China with his family and more than 20 people who had been infected by God's call to China. While living in China, the Taylor family faced many hardships: his daughter died from water on the brain; they were almost killed in the Yang Chow Riot of 1868; his first wife died in childbirth; and his second wife died of cancer. Nevertheless, China Inland Mission continued to press forward in spreading the name of Jesus throughout China. By 1895, the mission had 641 missionaries and 462 Chinese helpers at 260 stations. Under Hudson Taylor's leadership, China Inland Mission had supplied over half of the Protestant missionary force in China. By the time Hudson Taylor died in 1905, there were 205 missionary stations with 849 missionaries and 125,000 Chinese Christians in the China Inland Mission, and Taylor had spent five years on the translation of the New Testament into the Ningpo dialect.[6]

I also heard of a man who lived in a village in India in the 1900s. He was the only Christian in his village of 1,000 people. This man was consumed with the cause of Christ to the point that he made a vow to share who Christ was and is with every family in his village before he died. He accomplished this task. While he may not have seen a Jesus revolution in his village, he did see his son go on to study theology and, through his teaching, impact thousands of students for Jesus.

Against the Odds

Hudson Taylor and this Indian father are powerful examples of being consumed! We should additionally consider Paul, at the end of his life, in the middle of a shipwreck. Everyone on the boat was about to lose their lives due to a terrible storm (see Acts 27:21-24). Even toward the conclusion of his life, Paul did not quit the cause of Christ. In fact, he stood up on the boat in the middle of everyone and told them of God's power to rescue everyone on the ship. He didn't quit, even in very dark times.

In an even more powerful illustration, at the end of his life, Paul served Christ as a prisoner in the city of Rome. The prison was a horrible place. Historians tell us that this prison was actually part of the sewage system for the city of Rome. Raw sewage would run through it, ranging from ankle-deep to waist-deep. Paul was chained to a wall, with his hands over his head while the sewage would flow around his body and mice and rats would crawl over him.[7] In this setting, Paul was given the opportunity, as a Roman citizen, about once a month to write letters. It was during one of these opportunities that he wrote Philippians 3:8-9:

What is more, I consider everything a loss compared to the surpassing greatness of knowing Christ Jesus my Lord, for whose sake I have lost all things. I consider them rubbish, that I may gain Christ and be found in him....

In the middle of sewage, Paul said that whatever he had gained, or could have gained, was nothing more than sewage compared to knowing Jesus! Paul was consumed with knowing Christ.

On the Damascus road, in Acts chapter 9, Paul found a cause worth dying for. What about our world? Can you think of people you know who are devoted to a cause to the point of laying down their lives? What about some of the teens who died in the Columbine High School massacre, such as Cassie Bernal and Rachel Scott? Were they perfect in living out their Christianity? Absolutely not. But when it came down to being consumed with Jesus, there was no question—they gave their lives for Jesus.

Another example of someone I know who is consumed by the cause of Christ is my mother, Marilyn Hickey. When we lived in Kansas City, mom was planning a crusade in Pakistan. This was in the early 1990s, and there was all kinds of political volatility, violence, and some terrible things happening there. I called her to ask if she really thought it was prudent at that time to consider a crusade in that region of the world. I continued and expressed my concern that she could be killed for presenting such a public meeting for Jesus. She responded that it would be great to die in Pakistan because she would die a martyr's death. I remember her saying, "Do you realize that God would get more glory out of my death as a martyr than He would if I just kind of fizzled out and lived a sideline Christianity? I'd love to die as a martyr." She is consumed by the cause of Jesus.

Application

Let's try to make this a little more practical for your world. Let's come back again and think some more about what being consumed by the cause of Christ looks like in your life. When I talk about being consumed by the cause of Christ, I'm really asking if your default thinking reverts back to Jesus. When I say default thinking, I'm making a parallel to computer functions. For example, if you are working on a computer and after a while you take a break to answer the phone, after a while the computer screen will probably default to a screensaver. This is an automatic function within your computer—what it reverts to—its base level.

So look at how this applies to Jesus. What is your base level—what is your screensaver? Is Jesus your screensaver, so to speak? Has your life become so corrupted with Jesus that He's the first person you look to when you have a problem or a crisis? Has your life become so corrupted for Christ that you can't help but share how wonderful Jesus is? What about the people in your neighborhood, apartment complex, or dormitory? What about the person who gets on your nerves and you try to avoid? Can you make an adjustment to default to see them through the love that God has for them? Does your screensaver come up and say, "I'm so in love with Jesus that I want my neighbor to know how amazing He is? What screensaver comes up when a person cuts you off when you're driving to work? What is your default behavior toward the person who lives in the dorm room next to you or who works in the adjacent cubicle and has pornography all over his walls? What screensaver comes up when you find out that your neighbor is a Buddhist, Muslim, or Hindu? Are you in love with Jesus enough to be concerned about her eternity? Have you been consumed by the cause?

Another illustration: My husband and I now have three absolutely incredible children, whom I deeply love! When I was pregnant, much of my thinking went to taking care of my body better than normal because I had someone else's life to consider. When my children were newborns, my life was virtually consumed with caring for each beautiful treasure—I was living for another. My waking, my sleeping, my eating, my energies, and my tasks were almost completely devoted to the life of this new bundle of awesome life. Even though my children are bigger now, and we have moved beyond the baby phase in our family, I still find myself defaulting to my kids. If my kids are out of sorts, then I'm out of sorts. If they're sick or upset, I'm unsettled. Before I go to bed each night, I check on them to make sure they're OK. When I know that they're all settled in and sleeping well, then I can sleep restfully. I think that in some ways, the parental care we have toward our children is reflective of our heavenly Father passion for us. And I think it deeply pleases Him when we pick up His heart for people and devote our lives to turning our world upside down through His power and love.

Excuse Evasion

I quit high school. One of our best friends is a pastor from Australia. He's a first-rate pastor, and God has used him in ways far beyond his natural abilities. Thankfully, our friend didn't limit God based on his talents. You see, our friend has a learning disability that makes reading books really hard for him, and he is also a high school drop-out. Nevertheless, he is very engaged in accomplishing God's will in his life.

He understood the principle behind these words from *Campus Life* magazine in 1979, "Knowledge is exploding at such a rate—more than 2000 pages a minute—that even Einstein couldn't keep up. In fact, if you read 24 hours a day, from age 21 to 70, and retained all you read, you would be one and a half million years behind when you finished."[8] We can never be adequate on our own, but God gives us the power to be salt and light in the world. "Salt is good, but if it loses its saltiness, how can it be made salty again? It is fit neither for the soil nor for the manure pile; it is thrown out..." (Luke 14:34-35). As Martin Luther King Jr. said, "In this revolution, no plans have been written for retreat."[9]

Chapter 7

REALITY MEETS REVOLUTION

application—from the old French word *aplier*;
"to attach to, to devote oneself to";
"to bring things in contact with one another"[1]

Authentically caring for people is, in many ways, the Jesus revolution put to feet and applied in our daily living. Sincerely caring for people is counter-culture and perhaps even counter-human. Consider what happened on the Titanic, a luxury ocean liner that catered to wealthy people. On the night when it began to sink, there were many different reactions from people on the boat related to getting into the life boats. Some didn't believe that the ship was sinking because the advertising for the boat said that it was unsinkable. Some of the first-class passengers refused to let people into their lifeboats for fear that they might get overloaded and risk their own survival. Consequently, many of the Titanic's lifeboats, which were designed to hold up to 60 people, were rescued with only 15 people— while hundreds died a frozen and unnecessary death. Sometimes, I think Christians can be a little bit like the first-class passengers on the Titanic. We have the saving grace and knowledge to help us through life, but we don't share it with anyone because we don't want to rock our boat.

Rice Paddy Revolutionary

So where do we go from here? How do we live the revolutionary life that a Christian is designed to live? We've walked through the steps of turning our world upside down:

- Concerned about the cause.

- Confronted by the cause.

- Compelled by the cause.

- Corrupted by the cause.

- Consumed by the cause.

But now where do we go? We know that God wants to use us to turn our worlds upside down. But sometimes this line of thinking can be overwhelming. If it wasn't overwhelming, you probably would have already done it! It's important to understand that by yourself, living a revolutionary life is virtually impossible, but living upside down isn't impossible with God! In fact, with God's help, nothing is impossible. Living a revolutionary life without God is extremely hard. Living a revolutionary life *with God* is more than possible—it's **probable**! Let's think about your world—your city or town, your neighborhood, your workplace, your school, your grocery store, your commute to work, the gym where you work out, your dormitory, the hobby-related club you belong to, etc. When you think about turning all of this upside down for Jesus, it can be somewhat intimidating.

Here's an interesting story that may put some of this into perspective. We talked earlier about how the Viet Minh fought off the French in the Indochina War, culminating in the battle at Dien Bien Phu. There's another example I want to share with you that happened in the American phase of the Vietnam War. As you read this, please understand that I deeply value and appreciate the sacrifice of our men and women in Vietnam. This story is in no way a glorification of the conflict in Vietnam or an endorsement of the political struggles and outcomes from this era in American history. I am simply using this as an example of how we can turn our world upside down when a regular person becomes consumed by a cause.

In a Vietnamese village, there was a girl who worked in the rice paddies. She didn't have any major or formal military training, but she knew that she didn't want the Americans in her country. So, as she was working in the rice paddies, she noticed that there were American military planes that would fly over on a daily basis. Now this girl was just an average person, a farmer. She began to notice that as she watched the planes flying over her rice paddy, there was a pattern to these flights, as well as a pattern of timing. From this general observation, she started to take notes. After a while, she knew exactly all of the air maneuvers that were happening over her area. She took the notes that she had accumulated on these flight patterns and then gave them to a Vietnamese General, explaining her discoveries. From this information, the Vietnamese were able to shoot down several American planes, based on the observations of a farm girl in a rice paddy. She was a revolutionary. She turned her world upside down because she watched, she was engaged, and she was committed to her cause. She was a rice paddy revolutionary.[2]

Now if a female rice paddy farmer can do that for her nation, not to mention the nameless men who carried artillery parts up many hills to help drive the French out of Vietnam—if these average people can do that for their nation, what about us? What can we do for eternity? If the Vietnamese could fight so ardently and strongly, can we fight for the human eternities that live in our world? I'm not saying that we all need to become militaristic or formalized about the people in our neighborhood, workplace, gym, or school. I am saying that all we need to do is be Jesus with skin. What does it mean or look like to be Jesus with skin?

Fill Your Skin with Jesus

There are many people throughout history who have been Jesus with skin. Consider George Muller from the 1800s. As a child and teenager, he was a rowdy fellow. He partied hard and goofed off with his friends more than his dad liked. When he attended university, some friends invited him to a church meeting in a home where he continued to visit until he became a thoroughly turned-on believer in Jesus. From the time of his early 20s until his death at 93, he was both tireless and creative in promoting Christ in any way he could. By the end of his life, through an organization that he founded and managed, he and his wife had cared for more than 100,000 orphans in England. He also traveled extensively as a missionary, pastored the same church for more than 65 years, performed follow-up work for D.L. Moody, and inspired missionaries around the world, including Hudson Taylor.[3] All of this was a result of some of his friends inviting him to a home church meeting. We don't remember the names of George Muller's friends, who were just regular people, but we certainly do celebrate the extraordinary achievements that God did through Muller's life.

How about Paul Hewson? Could he be considered a person who lives like Jesus with skin? You may know him better as Bono, the lead singer for U2. Being such a public figure, Bono attracts lots of praise and criticism. But consider his upbringing. Born and raised in Ireland, his dad was a Catholic postal worker and his mom was a Protestant. Religion is a very controversial subject in predominately Catholic Ireland, and he was raised as a Protestant, even though neither the Catholic nor Protestant churches were very open to him since he came from a "mixed" marriage. His mom died unexpectedly when he was 14, and from that point on, he was a fairly rough kid who never quite connected with his dad. U2 started when a schoolmate posted a notice on the school bulletin board seeking musicians to join his band. From there, the band members of U2 worked hard, and they hit the charts early with tremendous success, which continue today, several decades later.

Bono is an interesting celebrity who never pretends to be anything but human. Despite his humanity, he uses his platform as a celebrity for some very revolutionary causes and does so very effectively. He has worked diligently over more than a decade to improve the living conditions of people around the world who don't have access to health care, education, political participation, or the power to improve themselves or their living conditions. Whether you agree or disagree with his beliefs, it's difficult to argue with his humanitarian values.[4]

Maybe you think that being Jesus with skin is too complicated for you. I heard a story from Joel Osteen about a disabled man who attended Joel's church for many years using the mass transit system in Houston. When the church moved into the former Compaq Center, the bus routes didn't allow the disabled man to continue going to church. So rather than sit and be discouraged, he began a campaign to convince the transit authorities to develop the necessary bus routes for his community to continue attending Joel's church at the Compaq Center. He wrote letters and e-mails, made phone calls, visited with political leaders, and used every means possible to voice his concern. Finally, there was a vote to improve the bus routes, thanks to this man's efforts; and now the necessary transit support exists, enabling this man and the community in which he lives to regularly attend church at the Compaq Center.[5] That's another expression of Jesus with skin. Similar to how Jesus made the sacrifice to connect us to our heavenly Father, this man made the sacrifice, through his work, commitment, and time for others in his community to be able to attend church weekly and make a stronger and deeper connection to their heavenly Father.

So what about you? What are some ways that you can be Jesus with skin? Here are some simple suggestions. You can be Jesus with skin by offering to pray for a co-worker who just shared that he's going through a divorce. You can be Jesus with skin by checking in with your neighbors to see how they're doing. You can offer to help a classmate with homework (not with a romantic or dating motivation). You can offer to help when you see someone in need at a grocery store or at the gym. When you begin to be consumed by the cause of Jesus and the effort to share His love in practical ways, you'll see the opportunities to be Jesus with skin become almost limitless. We must begin to engage with the people in our world in practical and living ways and let Jesus come out of our hearts and into our communities, one life at a time. We let Jesus use our skin to connect those around us to the reality, power, and practicality of His love.

Crawling Skin—Avoid It!

Let me also tell you how to make someone's skin crawl—be a hypocrite. Jesus talked about hypocrites and their ineffective lives in an entire chapter devoted to the religious leaders and Pharisees, a special group of Jewish men zealous about maintaining adherence to the Jewish law (see Matt. 23). In verses 13-15, Jesus confronted the *people skills* of the Pharisees and religious leaders—the most obvious place to spot a hypocrite. Jesus explained that the hypocrites of His day were arrogant in their interactions with people. When they were supposed to be helping people get into God's Kingdom, they were actually closing the door on anyone who tried to get in! Maybe you've caught yourself thinking that one of your neighbors isn't good enough to be a Christian—this would be the same trap that the Pharisees fell into.

Additionally, they victimized widows instead of helping them. Instead of assisting society's most vulnerable members, they took advantage of their lack of power and used it for their own benefit (see Matt. 23:1-30). This would be like using the weak, or someone less fortunate than yourself, to advance your position or status in life. The Pharisees flaunted their religious positions by their lengthy prayers. Their piety was a medal of honor that they paraded in order to strengthen their own positions in society (see Matt. 23:5-7). This would be like seeing yourself as more important than someone else because of the church you attend or your position in that church.

Finally, Jesus confronted the Pharisees and religious leaders about their people skills when they would make a convert. Jesus said that the converts that they made were like a "son of hell" (see Matt. 23:15). Their converts were followers of their religious dogma more than followers of God. Another topic that Jesus confronted these men on was their *values* (see Matt. 23:16-24). Simply put, the Pharisees and religious leaders justified their disobedience. They would be sure to watch out for the smallest details in keeping the law but ignore the bigger and more important issues like being people of their word (keeping their integrity), working for justice, giving mercy, and being faithful in their hearts toward God.

I think we can see the same problems today in Christianity. Do you ever play these mental games with yourself? *If I party Friday night, then I'll go to church Sunday to make up for it.* Or how about this one? *I didn't really have sex with her. It was just....* How about the mercy question? Do you find yourself naturally giving people what they "deserve," or are you generous with being kind, patient, and merciful?

One day after presenting leadership training in Berlin, Germany, I ate dinner with our hosts at a downtown café. After our meal, it was starting to get dark, so we decided to walk back to our car. As we were walking, I wasn't paying attention to where I was going, and I almost ran into a lady who looked kind of strange. She was wearing these really spiky high boots, and she had squeezed her torso into something like a corset so that her waist was probably about 15 inches around. I did a double take and looked at her because I thought that she was probably really uncomfortable in such strange looking clothes, and then it hit me—she was a hooker. Then as we kept walking, we began to see more and more prostitutes, and my heart began to go out to them. They seemed empty and hollow. I still wonder if anyone has made an effort to reach out to them with Jesus' love, no strings attached. A religious person would want to immediately leave and stay away from being corrupted. A revolutionary would say, "There, but for the grace of God, go I."[6]

Finally, Jesus confronted the Pharisees and religious leaders about their private world (see Matt. 23:25-28). In these verses, Jesus said that these men would tell everyone that it was OK to drink from a cup as long as the outside was clean. He also talked about how these leaders would go to extensive lengths to make sure everyone knew where a tomb or grave was by whitewashing it (so they could stay pure to share in Passover)—painting bright white lime all over the tomb or grave so that no one would touch it, even though the inside held a rotting, maggot-eaten cadaver. The outside of the Pharisees looked great, but the inside of their hearts were filled with all kinds of filth and wicked thoughts.

We need to be careful not to fall into the same traps as the men Jesus was confronting. Only you can know what goes on in your heart and your thoughts, what you let your emotions gravitate toward—but be guaranteed that whatever you allow to happen on the inside of you, will eventually make their way out to be observed by those around you.

It Starts in the Heart

Notice that Jesus worked His way backward in confronting these religious leaders. He talked about how they interacted with people, which was based upon the values they chose to live by, which in turn was based upon the private life in their hearts and minds. Revolution starts in the heart and works its way out—it always has and it always will.

In our world, an over-the-top example of a Christian hypocrite was the Church Lady on *Saturday Night Live*, played by Dana Carvey. In these sketches, the Church Lady was a pious, self-righteous, church attendee who would interview famous celebrities and then proceed to berate the guest for their "secular" living. Her attitude was one of condescension, arrogance, and total disregard for the human she was trying to humiliate. Dana Carvey said that he based the character for the Church Lady on some women from his church when he was growing up. What a sad commentary on who people think Christians are.

These sketches were hilarious, but they were also painful to watch, because I've seen people who call themselves Christians behave with the same attitudes and actions as the Church Lady and, consequently, become a total turn-off to anyone even mildly interested in Christianity.

Because Christians have behaved so poorly, it is becoming increasingly common to hear that someone is a follower of Jesus but they deny being a Christian. No one likes a hypocrite, but a hero is an ordinary person who goes beyond himself. Do this, with God's help, and your world will never be the same. My prayer for you is that you would be even more committed to the cause of Christ than the Viet Minh were committed to the cause of freedom—for truly we are fighting for the freedom of ourselves and humanity from the slavery of sin!

Excuse Evasion

I'm not married, or *I'm divorced*. Now this excuse seems really grounded because, of course, if you look around, almost everyone is married. However, God has always used single people in His work. Consider that Paul himself wasn't married. He also had a lot to say about singleness and marriage in First Corinthians 7:8-38.

I would like you to be free from concern. An unmarried man is concerned about the Lord's affairs—how he can please the Lord. But a married man is concerned about the affairs of this world— how he can please his wife— and his interests are divided. An unmarried woman or virgin is concerned about the Lord's affairs: Her aim is to be devoted to the Lord in both body and spirit. But a married woman is concerned about the affairs of this world—how she can please her husband. I am saying this for your own good, not to restrict you, but that you may live in a right way in undivided devotion to the Lord (1 Corinthians 7:32-35).

These verses show that God uses single people as well as married people. Being a revolutionary doesn't depend on your marital status.

Chapter 8

REVOLUTION ESSENTIALS

value—from the Latin word *valere*;
"be strong, be well, be of value"[1]

So we're going to turn our worlds upside down, and we're really excited about that. But maybe you're reading this and you're interested in knowing some core values that you'll need to perpetuate this revolution in your life so that the revolution isn't just a passing fancy. In all honesty, no one does anything of lasting worth without having values to go with their actions. In fact, if you look at your life today, you could probably figure out what your values are by the way you spend your time and money. But let's look at values as the anchor that holds your "boat" of life in position. Winds blow; seasons change; crises happen. What are the values that you return to and that shape your life?

Values Anchor Life

I had an interesting experience recently that gave me some unique insight into myself. I was preparing for a sermon that I was going to preach, and I needed to find a book that I had read about 25 years ago. This book had had a significant impact on my life for a season, and I wanted to go back and find it. So I went to the basement where we keep our storage stuff, and I began to go through various boxes looking for this book. As I went through all these different boxes, I found lots of interesting things, including some school work, personal mementos that had meaningful memories, and many journals. This brief walk down memory lane helped me see God's hand in my life at the various stages that I've been through. It helped me see that I've always had a hunger for God and that God's hand has been on my life, guiding me even in the most ungodly times of my life. It helped me see that I've always had a passion for God, whether it was a small ember or an all-consuming fire.

This adventure into my storage boxes helped me see that I've always valued a personal relationship with Jesus—this has been an anchor in my life. God has given me this value—it's absolutely nothing that I have concocted or rustled up. I'm sure that my mom and her prayers have been instrumental in maintaining this value—but beyond that, I believe that God has worked His way into my life, throughout its various seasons and despite my grotesque humanity, to give me this core value. My personal relationship with Jesus is central to my existence, and without this relationship, I am anchorless.

I believe that Paul was also very anchored in his relationship with Jesus. One of the most magnetic things that Paul ever wrote, which has appealed to me for almost 30 years, is Philippians 3:8-11:

What is more, I consider everything a loss compared to the surpassing greatness of knowing Christ Jesus my Lord, for whose sake I have lost all things. I consider them rubbish, that I may gain

Christ and be found in him, not having a righteousness of my own that comes from the law, but that which is through faith in Christ—the righteousness that comes from God and is by faith. I want to know Christ and the power of his resurrection and the fellowship of sharing in his sufferings, becoming like him in his death, and so, somehow, to attain to the resurrection from the dead.

Paul lived his life based on some very significant values, and at the end of his life, he said, "I have fought the good fight, I have finished the race, I have kept the faith," (2 Tim. 4:7).

True values stay with you, they guide you, they keep you, and they put ground under your feet as you walk this journey of life. An example of a person being guided by intrinsic values can also be seen in the history of the growth of Starbucks. If you read about this company, you'll note that one of its key leaders, Howard Schultz, has based his company and its operations on a system of simple core values. Schultz grew up in the projects of Brooklyn, New York, where his dad never really found his niche. As a blue collar, working class man, Schultz's dad had many jobs and had his fair share of negative working experiences. Schultz says that he never saw his dad receive dignity from his work.

Seeing such a void, Schultz has endeavored to integrate the core value of employee dignity in the workplaces of Starbucks, regardless of anyone's position in the organization. As evidence of this value of employee dignity, consider that Starbucks offers health insurance and employee ownership options to all of its employees, including part-time employees. This is an extremely rare practice.

We live in a day when companies are trying to minimize their costs, cut back on benefits, and look for ways to justify decreasing their expenses at the cost of their employees. There are even some companies who are eliminating health insurance coverage for their full-time employees. In contrast, Howard Schultz fundamentally believes that work should contribute dignity to one's sense of self and has transformed that belief into a core value in the operations of his worldwide organization. As a result of Starbuck's dedication to this value, the employee turn-over ratio is less than half of its largest competitor. Schultz's values have revolutionized the coffee shop industry.[2] In a time when many companies are struggling to keep their employees, Starbucks has retained its employees through staying true to its founding values.

What core values do we need to turn our worlds upside down? As individuals, what values should define our lives?

Values of a Jesus Revolution

A Jesus revolution needs Jesus' values. So what do these values include? Let's look at Jesus' teachings to explore the values He promoted. When you look at the entirety of what Jesus taught, He summarized His teachings into two main action points which would be the central values around which He built His revolution (see Matt. 22:37-39):

1. Love the Lord your God with all your heart, mind, soul, and strength.

2. Love your neighbor as yourself.

Simply put, we must make loving God the first priority in our lives, and after that, we must love those around us. These two action points completely connect to the way that we relate to God and others. In the simplest evaluation, Jesus speaks to what should be the basis of our relationships—love.

Loving God is the first value that Jesus spoke of. In all honesty, I think this is the easiest value to live out. The reason that this value is easy for us to live out is because it is the natural response to God's love for us. In First John 4:19, it says, "We love Him because He first loved us." His love for you is always first in your life, regardless of how you feel or what's happening around you.

I pray that you would have a deep experience with God's love for you—it is a central necessity to being transformed into the revolutionary that God wants you to be. Reflect back and consider the intensity and immensity of God's love for you—a love so strong and deep that He was willing to be publicly humiliated, to die in the most inhumane way, to be separated from His Father, and to experience isolation that none of us could comprehend. He did all of this based upon His love for us, so that we could be with Him eternally in a deep, heart-level relationship.

Think of the person in this world who loves you the most. Jesus' love for you exceeds this person's love for you so massively that words would limit the truth and expression of His love for you. So our natural response to such a love is obvious—to love Him back. I pray that love would be the premise of your relationship with God—His love for you and your love for Him. Nothing else will sustain your relationship with God better than love, and I believe that this is why Jesus gave us this value first.

Jesus quickly follows up on the value of loving God, and explains that we are also to love one another. In the past, this had been a difficult value for me. In my growing-up years, I had seen people hurt each other and had experienced people hurting me at school, in my neighborhood, at church, and basically anywhere humans could interact. Thus, I didn't feel any strong desire to "love my neighbor as myself." I had no problem loving God—that was easy. But when it came to loving *people*, that was another matter altogether.

One day, however, I had been working on memorizing First John. I really enjoy memorizing because I feel like it draws me closer to God and helps me know Him better. So as I was memorizing, I came to First John 4:20-21 where it says:

If anyone says, "I love God," yet hates his brother, he is a liar. For anyone who does not love his brother, whom he has seen, cannot love God, whom he has not seen. And he has given us this command: Whoever loves God must also love his brother.

God began to speak to me and confront me about my thinking and attitudes about loving others. He showed me that loving Him is equivalent to loving others. If I don't love my neighbors, then I don't love Him. You can't separate the two. They are mutually interdependent. Consequently, God has really helped change my heart toward people, and I believe that He is still helping me to live out the love that I have for Him with the people who are in my life on all levels.

The Value of Love

So what is love, and what does it look like? Is it the Valentine we give to someone on February 14? Is it when I make my husband's favorite German chocolate cake? Is it when I see a mom in a grocery store trying to juggle a baby in a car seat, a shopping cart, and two other children—and I help her? What is love? Love is not limited to an emotion, a state of the mind, or an action. Love is described in First Corinthians 13:4-7:

> *Love is patient, love is kind. It does not envy, it does not boast, it is not proud. It is not rude, it is not self-seeking, it is not easily angered, it keeps no record of wrongs. Love does not delight in evil but rejoices with the truth. It always protects, always trusts, always hopes, always perseveres.*

What are some things that love is and does? It is patient and kind. Love does rejoice in truth; it *always* protects, trusts, hopes, and perseveres.

The power of love and its positive out-workings are easily seen in the medical practices of the Menninger Clinic. In the early 1900s, a father and his two sons who had graduated from medical school started a mental institute in Kansas. At this time, the solution for mental patients was to basically farm them out to a cold and impersonal institution for their entire lives. The Menningers, however, had a different strategy. These men believed that, if their staff would express value and love for their patients, they could reverse many mental disorders. This revolutionary method became world famous, and Karl Menninger, one of the brothers and the founders of the Menninger Clinic, said:

> Love cures people—both the ones who give it and the ones who receive it. This intangible thing—love—enters into every therapeutic relationship. It is an element which finds and heals, which comforts and restores, which works what we have to call for now, miracles.[3]

This helps us see what love is and what love can accomplish, but what are some things that love is *not* in First Corinthians chapter 13? It is *not* proud, rude, self-seeking, or easily angered; love does not envy, boast, keep a record of wrongs, or delight in evil. Martin Luther King Jr. contrasted the powers of love and hate in his sermon "Loving your enemies." He was imprisoned at the time for promoting equal rights for African Americans. We know that Martin Luther King Jr. received multiple death threats aimed at him, his family, and those who were closest to him. He was also accused of being a Communist, his house was bombed, and he was jailed more than 20 times. Yet, in this sermon, he said "hate multiplies hate...in a descending spiral of violence" and is "just as injurious to the person who hates" as it is to his victim. But "love is the only force capable of transforming an enemy into a friend" for it has "creative" and "redemptive" power.[4]

So we see that love must be a core value in being a Jesus revolutionary. Love is a guiding principle to our hearts and in our relationships. I believe that love is the most central and core value around which God will use us to revolutionize our worlds. Everything in our revolution works its way out as an expression of the central value of love.

The Vision of Revolution

A successful revolution needs not only a set of values, but it also needs vision. What does a revolutionary look like? When we think about revolutionaries, maybe you conjure up in your mind pictures of people who negatively revolutionized their worlds: Fidel Castro, Lenin, Eminem, Osama bin Laden, or others. If you're like me, none of these figures are particularly appealing. If I told you that you had to be like them to turn your world upside down, you'd probably stop reading right here. Please don't quit now—God has a different path for you to take in revolutionizing your world. Whew! In fact, Isaiah 55:9 says that God does things a lot differently than we do.

When I think back through my life, I can see that God has done some absolutely amazing things in ways that I never thought He would! As I grew up, people always said to me, "You're going to grow up and teach the Bible just like your mom." My response under my breath was, "drop dead!" The last thing in the world that I wanted to do was teach the Bible like my mom! Now don't misunderstand me. I love my mom and dad, and they've been wonderful parents to me. My resistance to teaching the Bible like my mom didn't come out of a sense of rebellion or anger with my parents. Rather, I wanted to be an individual—to be myself and not to live in anyone's shadow. I wanted to pave my own road and not travel in someone else's groove.

I've always had a strong sense of individuality that has sometimes interfered with what God wanted to accomplish. Nevertheless, my individuality was strong even when I was five years old and determined I was going to be an astronaut. When I was 12 years old, I was going to be an archeologist, and in college I was going to be a nuclear physicist. I wanted to be really smart! I had all these ideas of what I was going to be, and thankfully, God had different ideas—good different ideas!

Turning the world upside down requires the right perspective—the right vision. We need to have God's viewpoint. Think about Balaam in the Bible (see Num. 22). He was really ticked off at his donkey because the donkey kept doing the opposite of what Balaam wanted him to do. Balaam wanted him to stay on the road, and the donkey wandered off. Balaam was in a narrow ravine, and the donkey crushed his foot against the wall. Finally, the donkey laid down under him and refused to go any more. By this point, Balaam was furious and started to beat his donkey. In response, his donkey began to talk back to him and asked why he was being beaten. The donkey then explained that the reason why he had been behaving so badly was because an angel was blocking his path. Balaam didn't see the angel, but the donkey did.

In another example, Elisha and his servant were surrounded by an enemy army trying to capture and kill Elisha (see 2 Kings 6). Now Elisha wasn't even close to nervous, but his servant was completely off the freak-out chart. So Elisha prayed and asked God to open his servant's eyes; and after this prayer, his servant could see the army of God all over the hills surrounding the village, and he was no longer afraid. Vision determines where we go.

Think about this story:

Dinner was over, and Jimmy was playing, while Mom and Dad were absorbed with jobs and didn't notice the time. It was a full moon, and some of the light seeped through the windows. Then Mom glanced at the clock. "Jimmy, it's time to go to bed. Go up now, and I'll come and settle you later." Unlike usual, Jimmy went straight upstairs to his room.

An hour or so later, his mother came up to check if all was well, and to her surprise found that her son was staring quietly out of his window at the moonlit scenery.

"What are you doing, Jimmy?"

"I'm looking at the moon, Mommy."

"Well, it's time to go to bed now."

As one reluctant boy settled down, he said, "Mommy, you know one day I'm going to walk on the moon."

Who could have known that the boy in whom the dream was planted that night would survive a near fatal motorbike crash which broke almost every bone in his body, and would realize this dream 32 years later when James Irwin stepped on the moon's surface?[5]

Vision is essential. Living without God's perspective will only limit what He can do through you. Consider the Italian sculptor Agostino d'Antonio who worked diligently on a large piece of marble. Unable to produce his desired masterpiece, he lamented, "I can do nothing with it." Other sculptors also worked this difficult piece of marble, but to no avail. Michelangelo discovered the stone and visualized the possibilities in it, creating from it one of the world's masterpieces—*David*.[6]

If we try to turn our worlds upside down by looking at our environments from our viewpoint and not God's viewpoint, we're only going to make things worse. Again, His ways are not our ways (see Isa. 55:9). Truly, if we begin to live life from God's perspective, we will live an upside-down life—upside down in relation to the world in which we live.

Our world tells us that to be successful we have to be sharp, we have to be smart, and we have to be better than everyone else. We have to think better, be more positive, be more in shape, and be stronger than everyone else. The list goes on. According to God, these things are upside down to His definition of success. God's definition of and path to success, or an upside-down life, is different from the world's definition. The vision we have of our lives needs to be shaped by the values that God gives us. Without these values, without God's vision, we won't unlock the potential that God has put within each of us.

Excuse Evasion

I have kids. Now this excuse may seem to be the most significant. After all, our kids are some of the most important people in our lives. Really, they're our link to the future. As such, I think it is all the more important to live a revolutionary life *because* of our children! Think about the possibilities highlighted in the following illustration:

> Celeste Sibley, one-time columnist for the *Atlanta* (Georgia) *Constitution*, took her three children to a diner for breakfast one morning. It was crowded, and they had to take separate seats at the counter. Eight-year-old Mary was seated at the far end of the counter, and when her food was served, she called down to her mother in a loud voice, "Mother, don't people say grace in this place?" A hush came over the entire diner, and before Mrs. Sibley could figure out what to say, the counter-man said, "Yes, we do, sister. You say it." All the people at the counter bowed their heads. Mary bowed her head and in a clear voice said, "God is great, God is good, let us thank Him for our food."[7]

God's ways are higher and far superior to ours, as it says in Isaiah 55:9, "As the heavens are higher than the earth, so are my ways higher than your ways and my thoughts than your thoughts." Or, as Nicolas Copernicus, a 16th-century astronomer and mathematician, puts it in his declaration that humanity (Earth) is not the center of the universe: "Finally we shall place the Sun himself at the center of the Universe. All this is suggested by the systematic procession of events and the harmony of the whole Universe, if only we face the facts, as they say, 'with both eyes open.'"[8]

Chapter 9

REVOLUTION IN VALUES AND VISION

*B*ackward is an interesting word to consider in relation to revolution. Most revolutionaries believe that their efforts are progressive—that their actions are bringing progress to the world they live in. Revolutionaries generally don't think their causes are for backward momentum. *Backward* is an interesting word. It comes from the old English word abakward, and in 1535, it meant "behindhand with regard to progress"[1] In today's world, backward means "in reverse order" or "toward the past."

So is God backward? I've found that, more often than not, God doesn't do things the way I think He would. In fact, it seems like He does things in a topsy-turvy fashion—success God's way for God's results. Think again about Isaiah 55:8-9:

> *"For my thoughts are not your thoughts, neither are your ways my ways," declares the Lord. "As the heavens are higher than the earth, so are my ways higher than your ways and my thoughts than your thoughts."*

Is God's Revolution Backward?

This principle is well demonstrated in the story of Barak and Deborah in Judges chapter 4. Deborah was an Israelite leader during a time of relative instability in Israeli history. She summoned a man named Barak and told him to lead an army of Israelites against their enemy oppressors, promising that God would destroy the enemy. This sounds like a great plan, but what really happened turned out to be a very upside-down battle. What made this battle upside down? Well, to begin with, most wars are initiated by men. This battle, however, was instigated by a woman. This is very unusual. Furthermore, Barak received his "orders" from a woman. To top that off, Barak insisted that Deborah go into battle with him! This is all highly irregular—very upside down.

Since when did a man ever tell a woman that he needed her to go into battle with him? In our world, it's very controversial to have a woman in a fighting position, let alone co-leading a battle with a man! That's not the end, though. As you keep reading this upside-down story, you'll see that Deborah actually helped Barak recruit his soldiers (see Judges 4:9-10). Then, Deborah agreed to go with Barak, but explained that, because of the way he was going about this battle, the victory would come through a woman—again, highly irregular. Once they were ready, Barak waited for Deborah to give the signal to begin the battle. This is all extremely upside down—the opposite of what we would normally expect.

I want to stop a moment here and ask you to consider some of the struggles that you're currently going through in your life. Maybe you've been having a difficult time in your job or in a class. Maybe you're struggling with a teacher or an employer, or perhaps your marriage or health is going through a rough time. Have you tried to fix your struggles with your own ideas? Sometimes we have some great ideas, but I have found that more often than not, my own plans can really mess things up. Maybe that's why the world we live in is so messed up—because we've tried to sort things out without consulting God or allowing His intervention.

Maybe you have checked in with God but what He told you to do seems somewhat outlandish—maybe even upside down. We need to come to the realization that God's ways are higher than our ways and that His thoughts are higher than our thoughts. This puts Him on a different (higher) plane. Am I advocating abandoning your doctor's instructions or quitting that class that's so difficult? Absolutely not! What I am encouraging you to do is to seek God—something that our world is unfamiliar with—and to trust and obey Him. Quite simply, this is what Barak did. He trusted God and followed what God told him to do.

So what happened to Barak? He went to battle to fight against the Israelite enemy, Sisera, who came against Barak with 900 chariots. In Judges chapter 5, you'll read that there was a big flood and that all of Sisera's chariots that came out to fight got stuck in the mud! Again, that's unconventional—the chariots that were supposed to provide shock, awe, and overwhelming victory instead got "stuck in the mud" and turned into a detriment due to their immobility. Then Sisera, the enemy general, ran away from the battle and went into a lady's tent—Jael's tent. If you study Jael, you'll discover that she was the wife of Heber, who was friends with Sisera's boss. So when Sisera went into Jael's tent, he thought he would be safe hiding there.

In fact, when you read Judges 4:18, you'll see that Jael told Sisera to come into her tent and to not to be afraid! She covered him up with a blanket and gave him some milk and he laid down to rest. Obviously, he thought he was safe and protected. And why wouldn't he, considering all of these things he received from Jael? He even told her to stand guard at the door and to tell anyone who might inquire that no one was in her tent. Sisera trusted Jael. But remember, this is an upside-down battle, so literally anything could happen!

Judges 4:21 says, "But Jael, Heber's wife, picked up a tent peg and a hammer and went quietly to him while he lay fast asleep, exhausted. She drove the peg through his temple into the ground, and he died." She *nailed* him into the ground. Tell me *that's* not upside down. The battle against Sisera was not won on a battlefield, but in the tent of a woman who used a tent peg and a hammer. This went right along with what had God told Barak, through Deborah, about the victory of the battle. God had said that the battle wouldn't be won in the conventional manner, and He was absolutely right. Truly, God's ways are not our ways, and His thoughts are higher than our thoughts.

Consider Your Direction

So where does that leave us? How do we take the upside-down battle of Deborah and Barak and apply their lesson to our lives? The simplest way to relate this to our 24/7 is to consider Proverbs 3:5-6, "Trust in the Lord with all your heart and lean not on your own understanding; in all your ways acknowledge him, and he will make your paths straight."

Let me tell you a story I heard about God making straight paths in a really difficult situation. There was a Marine who was fighting in Iraq, and a huge sandstorm was coming. This Marine began to pray and ask God to make the sandstorm go away so that his platoon could safely return to their bunkers. God did not make the sandstorm go away; in fact, it got so bad that they had to set up a temporary camp and spend the night there, where the sandstorm continued to rage through the night. The next morning when they woke up, the Marine was frustrated with God, thinking that God hadn't answered his prayer. When he came out of his tent, he saw that the wind had blown the sand so hard through the night that it had cleared the road that they were going to use to get back to their bunkers. Now that the sand was blown away, they could see land mines on the road. God had protected the Marine and his platoon, but in an upside-down way.

So how does all of this connect to your life? How do you acknowledge God in all your ways, so that He can direct your paths, as it says in Proverbs 3:5-6? What does "in all my ways" mean? *Ways* in the Hebrew has six meanings. The first meaning is simply "route." This would mean the route that you take to get out of debt; the route that you take to have a good marriage; the route you take to find a mate; the route you take to pass a class or get a promotion. In all of the routes you take to get to a destination in your life, acknowledge God.

Next, *ways* means "distance." Essentially, distance is the space between two points. Sometimes the distance to your goal is short. Maybe your goal is to finish a school project, and you have one more meeting before its completion—that's a short distance. Maybe your goal is to get a promotion at work, and that seems so far away that you're tempted to try to take a shortcut. Remember, in all of your ways acknowledge God, and He will direct your path. Sometimes, as we pray to God, He shortens the distance, but I also think that there are times when the distance remains long so we will continue to depend on Him.

So far, if we're drawing a map of "in all our ways," we understand that our route to the destination is one of the "ways" that we acknowledge God. We're also to acknowledge God when we calculate the distance—be that long or short.

In our third meaning of *ways*, we learn that it means "journey" in Hebrew. Basically, the journeys are our daily minutes. The journey is the moment-by-moment plodding along that we do as we attempt to get closer to the goal. "Manner" is the fourth meaning for *way*. This word relates to our conduct and how we do things. In all of our conduct, mannerisms, and behaviors, we're to acknowledge God. Now that probably rubs you a little raw when you start to consider this applied to your life.

I read a story the other day about a woman in a car who was absolutely flipping out. She had the windows rolled down and was screaming and cussing out the driver in front of her, flipping off the driver, making rude gestures, and honking her horn. She was out of control. A cop pulled up behind her, observed her behavior, and immediately arrested her and took her to jail. You can imagine how she reacted to that! After several hours in jail, she calmed down, and the policeman who arrested her came to ask her some questions. She immediately asked him why she was arrested, to which he replied, "Ma'am, I arrested you because the car that you were driving had a 'Loving Jesus' bumper sticker, a license plate holder that read, 'Know Jesus, know peace; no Jesus, no peace,' a Cross hanging from the rearview window, and a chrome fish decal on the back of your car. I arrested you because clearly you stole that car!"[2]

In all of our conduct, we're to acknowledge God.

The fifth meaning of *ways* is "condition." This is how your journey shapes you along the road to your destination. The things that shape and mold us along the way can be either negative or positive. In all the things that mold you, you're to acknowledge God—and not in a cruel and blaming way. The last meaning of *ways* is "destiny," and it relates to our goals. Basically, God is saying that we are to acknowledge Him in all of our goals. What God is asking from us is not just a nod of the head to recognize Him. Rather, He is asking us to consult Him before we make our goals. He's asking us to get on His page first before we tell Him to get on our page—to get in sync with us. How many times have you gotten upset with God because He wasn't doing what you asked, and when you finally stopped to listen, He explained that He never had anything to do with your goal to start with? Destiny and goals— God wants us to acknowledge Him, to check in with Him *before* we set goals.

My Triathlon Way

Here's a great analogy to help you apply the differences of "acknowledging God in all your ways." I was in a few triathlons, short races that includes swimming, biking, and running. Let's look at how the six different meanings of "way" relate to the swimming part of my triathlons. First I had the *route* by which I had to swim. This route was mapped out by the buoys in the water. The *distance* I swam was .5 miles (not very long). My *journey* occurred as I swam—my progress as I swam along to get to my destination. In my training for the triathlons, I would swim indoors, and my pool had a black line at the bottom. My training was in a very static environment—it had virtually no waves, constant water temperature, and consistent visibility. I even often had an entire lane to myself. An open water swim is entirely different— there's no line at the bottom of the reservoir. It has a constantly chang-ing water temperature, lots of waves, and zero visibility. And lots of people would bump into me as I swam. So my manner of swimming, just to keep track of where I was going so that I didn't veer off course too badly, was to breast-stroke and freestyle—freestyle for the speed and breast-stroke for the visibility. That's a description of my journey.

The *manner* in which I swam was interesting compared to my co-athletes. Some athletes in the race were extremely competitive, and they let me know that from the beginning. They were intent on winning and were sure to let me know that they didn't want me in their way. As for me, my manner of racing, my behavior and conduct were different by comparison. In my race, I was racing to finish—swimming so I didn't drown. I wasn't racing to prove some colossal point, so I tended to be more laid-back and friendly. Now let's consider my *condition*—what shaped me in the swimming part of my race.

In one of my triathlons, they would let the racers begin in waves of 100 people. So there were eight to 10 groups of 100 athletes each who would hit the water every three to five minutes. Obviously, these are some large numbers of people to enter the water at the same time, and so it's not difficult to imagine that as I began to swim, I could easily get kicked by someone nearby, and just as easily, I could accidentally kick someone behind me. Consequently, when I came out of the water from finishing the swimming portion, I had several bruises.

Finally, the *destiny* aspect of my triathlon happened when I finished swimming and could feel mud under my feet as I began to run out of the reservoir.

What About You?

So after our discussion of the word *ways*, here are some questions for reflection: Are you acknowledging God in all of your ways? Are you acknowledging God in your ways even though it seems to be taking a long time? Are you acknowledging God along the journey, or have you thrown in the towel and decided to do it *your* way? Are you acknowledging God in your behavior along the way, or do you blow Him off when it gets tough or inconvenient to acknowledge Him? Are you acknowledging God on how your journey shapes you? Are you a bitter person because of your journey, or have you stayed tender despite some "mishaps"? Are you acknowledging God with the goals for your life? Are you acknowledging God with your yearly goals? Are you acknowledging God with even the things you'd like to accomplish this week? Has God come into the picture of your life for more than just the normal, "please help me do this," or "please bless this effort"?

In all honesty, if we're truly going to keep our faith in an upside-down world, we must sincerely acknowledge God in all our ways—not through mere lip service or frivolous Christianese banter. We must adopt, as our core value, the determination to allow God to take the reins of our life, to lead, direct, enact, and control our lives at His discretion. When we think about giving God control of our lives—letting Him have the final say, we are doing something revolutionary, according to our world and the times in which we live.

Let me tell you about some revolutionary people who lived and died for a great cause (though it was nothing like the cause of Christ). Fifty-six men signed the *Declaration of Independence* for the United States. Their conviction resulted in untold suffering for themselves and their families. Of the 56 men, five were captured by the British and tortured before they died. Twelve had their homes ransacked and burned. Two lost their sons in the Revolutionary Army. Another had two sons captured. Nine of the 56 fought and died from wounds or hardships of the war.

Carter Braxton of Virginia, a wealthy planter and trader, saw his ships sunk by the British navy. He sold his home and properties to pay his debts and died in poverty. At the battle of Yorktown, the British General Cornwallis had taken over Thomas Nelson's home for his headquarters. Nelson quietly ordered General George Washington to open fire on the Nelson home. The home was destroyed and Nelson died bankrupt. John Hart was driven from his wife's bedside as she was dying. Their 13 children fled for their lives. His fields and mill were destroyed. For over a year, he lived in forests and caves, returning home only to find his wife dead and his children vanished. A few weeks later, he died from exhaustion.[3]

These men were revolutionaries, and they turned their worlds upside down for political reasons. Their convictions ran deep. If we're going to turn our world upside down for eternal reasons, then our convictions and our values need to run even deeper. So how do we embrace such a great undertaking to effect eternal results? The answer rests in acknowledging God. Again, Proverbs 3:5-6 tells us that as we acknowledge God in all our ways, He will direct our paths. *Acknowledge* has three primary meanings: "to know by observing, reflecting or thinking; to know by experience; and to know so that you can give back."[4]

Let's Evaluate

Here's an exercise to help you evaluate your values. Listed below are the six definitions of *ways* that we talked about earlier. Take the three primary meanings of *acknowledge* and begin applying them to each of the following definitions:

1.   For example, let's take the first word, *route.*

Do you know God by observation along the route that you're taking? Do you know God by experience along the route that you're taking? Do you know God along the route that you're taking so much that you could teach someone about God because of what you've learned about Him through the route you're traveling?

2. Let's look at the second definition, *distance,* and do the same exercise.

Are you watching for God (observing Him) in the distance that you've traveled so far? What experience has shaped your understanding of God in the distance you've traveled? What could you teach someone else about God that you've learned so far, in the distance you've gone?

3. What about your *journey*—the daily moments?

Are you watching for God in a daily way along your journey? Can you identify some times when you have experienced God along your journey? What daily lessons have you learned about God that you could share with someone else?

4. How about your *conduct or manner*?

Does your conduct reflect your awareness of God? How have various experiences with God's presence affected your conduct? What could you share with someone else about how God has affected your conduct?

5. What about your *condition*?

How has your awareness of God shaped some of your negative experiences in life? Can you identify a time when your experience with God brought some great results out of a difficult situation? What are some lessons you could pass along from knowing God and allowing Him to shape you?

6.   Finally, what about your *destiny*?

Has your observation of God affected the destinies that you've chosen in life? If so, how? How have some of your experiences with God influenced your destiny? How would you coach someone in integrating God into their life's destiny?

These are incredibly powerful questions—they require a lot of reflection, honesty, and sincerity. Perhaps you'd like to consider one group of questions each day for the next six days in order to give each group a thorough time of digestion and to let God lead you as you answer. As you consider these questions and allow God to lead you in both your answers and applications, I truly believe that by giving God greater access to your life, you can be radically turned upside down.

Wherever you are in life, and wherever you are with God, increase your intake of God. Let's take Him on the route, on the journey with us. In our daily minutes, when we're riding the bus, getting up in the morning, drinking our coffee, studying for a test, picking up our kids, hanging out in our room, let's bring God with us. Let's not just go through the motions of life and lose track of God because of life's daily grind. God desperately wants to be on your journey of life. He wants your recognized inclusion. He wants you to experience Him even in the daily and mundane moments, not merely for the purpose of rules, but for the purpose of a deepening and vibrantly growing relationship with Him.

Excuse Evasion

I'm not strong enough. You may be thinking that you have to be this ultra-strong, powerful, charismatic, and commanding person to make a difference in your world. You may be a more quiet, reserved, and non-risky person, and may think that your personality isn't suitable for "revolutionary behavior." Maybe you just feel worn down by life and weak and tired with just trying to stay alive or keep your life together. I like the quote from Sonia Johnson, an out-spoken feminist and women's rights activist, when she said, "All bona-fide revolutions are of necessity revolutions of the spirit."[5]

Chapter 10

THE PLAN FOR REVOLUTION

change—from Celtic origin: *kamb*;
"to bend, crook"; "to make different"[1]

Revolution without Jesus is messy and temporary at best. An example of a tragic revolution was the cultural revolution in China in the 1960s and '70s. This revolution, from Mao Tse-tung's presentation, was to continue the revolt that had started about 15 years earlier with his sweep into power. This was a time when Mao could have been feeling politically vulnerable. To solidify his power, Mao had a strategy to confront any political opposition and consolidate his power to an even greater extent. In a very clever way, Mao did several things. To begin, he encouraged the youth of his nation to rise up and take greater control—to assert themselves and push forward the communist revolution with their young energy. He also strengthened his influence even more by his "re-education" plan. This strategy was to turn Chinese society upside down.

Mao attempted to accomplish this upheaval by sending to the countryside, or prison, as many of the intelligentsia that he could find throughout the nation. As such, doctors, lawyers, teachers, and anyone with education were sent away from their work to instead do heavy manual labor—most often farming. In their place, the peasants from the countryside were welcomed to take the vacancies of these educated people and to fill their roles and duties.

Even within his own government, Mao was ruthless. One of his most loyal followers, Zhou Enlai, was allowed to die of bladder cancer even though he could have been easily cured. You can see that such a plan would be thoroughly disastrous, and it was. Mao sent China into a very destructive tailspin. Anyone who opposed him was imprisoned or placed in positions where they would have no voice or opportunity to express themselves. When Mao died in 1976, he left a nation that was broken, with no clear plan of succession. China's cultural revolution was a failure at best. It was a human revolution that had bad human results.

On the flip side, let's continue to look at the Jesus revolution. The Jesus revolution has "un-human" results. Think about Galatians 5:22-23: "But the fruit of the Spirit is love, joy, peace, patience, kindness, goodness, faithfulness, gentleness and self-control. Against such things there is no law." These verses show us some of the results of the Jesus revolution that come out of our hearts. So how do we measure our progress in this Jesus revolution? Here are four ways to measure our progress, to see how fully this revolution has infused our lives:

Measure 1—You Live by Dying

Galatians 2:20 says, "I have been crucified with Christ and I no longer live, but Christ lives in me. The life I live in the body, I live by faith in the Son of God, who loved me and gave himself for me." If you want to be truly strong, to have authentic success, to have prosperity with peace, and to daily look at yourself in the mirror with fulfillment and contentment, then you must die to yourself and live to Christ. This means that you may need to make some adjustments on some of your paths. Maybe it's time for a "page check." Whose page are you mainly living on—yours or His? Can you say with Paul that you no longer live for yourself, but that you live for Jesus? That is truly revolutionary.

In my own life, I've found that the more I live for Jesus, the more fulfilled I am in my heart. The opposite is equally true. The more I try to fill myself with people, things, and activities, the more empty I am. In the past, I've struggled with co-dependency. This occurs when a person has an unhealthy dependency on another individual to the point of almost feeding off of the life of the other person. God has really dealt with me about this and about the source of this deception. He has spoken to me and shown me that the hole inside me was never designed to be filled by anyone but Him.

My past behavior was to find a person to fill that emptiness. Now, if I ever feel empty, it is a healthy reminder to find my life in Christ—fundamentally, and not through other relationships. For me, this has been a healthy paradigm shift. This isn't to say that I don't enjoy any close friendships or relationships—not at all. In fact, I've found that the more I center myself in Christ and look to Him to fill the gap, the better my external relationships have become. In this experience and in my way of thinking, I died to the old behavior patterns that were so destructive and found my life in Christ. I died, so that I can truly live. May I live to be more fully devoted to Jesus! Andrew Murray said, "God is ready to assume full responsibility for the life wholly yielded to Him."[2]

Measure 2—The Way Up is Down

We all want to be promoted and have great success in our lives. Everyone wants to be cool and at the top. But in James 4:10, the Bible says, "Humble yourselves before the Lord, and He will lift you up." So the question to ask yourself is, "who are you promoting?" Who does your life promote? Do you promote yourself more than Jesus? I believe that we can have a constructive amount of self-confidence. However, if we really want to succeed and excel in life, Jesus tells us that the way up is to go down. He tells us that we must humble ourselves and take the low road.

What does it mean to take the low road? The low road is when you look for opportunities to serve others, even those with whom you're competing. We look for ways to help our mates—husbands helping wives and wives helping husbands. We do that with our children, with our roommates, with our parents, with our friends and co-workers. This is another upside-down value. Here's a great example of what it means to take the low road:

> Shortly after Booker T. Washington, a renowned African American educator, took over the presidency of Tuskegee Institute in Alabama, he was walking in an exclusive section of town when he was stopped by a wealthy white woman. Not knowing the famous Mr. Washington by sight, she asked if he would like to earn a few dollars by chopping wood for her. Because he had no pressing business at the moment, Professor Washington smiled, rolled up his sleeves, and proceeded to do the humble chore she had requested. When he was finished, he carried the logs into the house and stacked them by the fireplace. A little girl recognized him and later revealed his identity to the lady.

The next morning, the embarrassed woman went to see Mr. Washington in his office at the Institute and apologized profusely. "It's perfectly all right, Madam," he replied. Occasionally I enjoy a little manual labor. Besides, it's always a delight to do something for a friend." She shook his hand warmly and assured him that his meek and gracious attitude had endeared him and his work to her heart. Not long afterward, she showed her admiration by persuading some wealthy acquaintances to join her in donating thousands of dollars to the Tuskegee Institute.[3]

Another good example of taking the low road happened in 1973 with Democratic Senator John Stennis in Washington DC. Senator Stennis, chairman of the Armed Forces Committee, was driving home after a long and tough day when two people snuck out of the dark, shot him two times, and robbed him in front of his house. He was immediately rushed to the hospital and was operated on for more than six hours. Another politician heard about Senator Stennis and rushed to the hospital to check on the Senator. When he arrived, he saw that the Senator's staff was swamped trying to keep up with the calls coming in enquiring about the Senator's condition. This politician quickly sat down at the switchboard which was unattended. He stayed at the switchboard all through the night and sometime in the next day, when everything quieted down, he gathered his coat and prepared to leave. Before walking away, he introduced himself to the switchboard operator as Mark Hatfield and let her know that he was happy that he could be helpful. Then, he quietly walked away.[4]

The other politician was Senator Hatfield, a Republican Senator. Under normal situations, a conservative Republican and a liberal Democrat rarely see eye-to-eye, let alone spend hours doing a menial task and being "happy to help out." These are both excellent examples of what it means to take the low road in life to find opportunities to help others in need.

In contrast, this is what can happen when we're unwilling to take the low road: In 1986, two ships crashed into each other off the coast of Russia. Unfortunately, several hundred passengers died, as they were plunged into the frigid waters of the Black Sea. The reason the two ships crashed wasn't due to weather or a technological difficulty. The accident occurred because the captains of the two ships were stubborn. They each knew that the other ship was close and both could have easily steered away from the other, but neither captain would yield to the other one until they finally ran into each other. These two ship captains played a dangerous game of "chicken" and the victims of their obstinacy paid with their lives.[5]

Measure 3—We Receive by Giving

Solomon was a very intelligent man. He wrote in Ecclesiastes 11:1, "Cast your bread upon the waters, for after many days you will find it again." Solomon said this even more clearly in Proverbs 11:24-25, "There is one who scatters, yet increases more; and there is one who withholds more than is right, but it leads to poverty. The generous soul will be made rich, and he who waters will also be watered himself" (NKJV). I've seen this axiom—that we receive by giving—to be true throughout my life, and I'll bet you can think of times when you were grateful that you had behaved generously. Can you think of some times when you were stingy and you regretted it? Our world is full of stingy people. To be the Jesus revolution, we must be counter-cultural.

Consider this story about Alexander the Great—king of Macedonia and considered one of the greatest generals in history. Alexander was taking a walk one day, when a beggar alongside the road asked the great king for some coins. Of course Alexander owed this beggar nothing, but he generously threw him several gold coins. One of Alexander's servants who was walking with him was surprised at his generosity and said that a few pennies would have been more than enough for the beggar. Interestingly, Alexander explained that while copper coins would be adequate for the needs of the beggar, gold coins are more fitting for the giving of such a great leader as himself.[6]

This illustration is a great example of generosity as a lifestyle. It's an even better example of the generosity of our heavenly Father toward us. Generosity is the way to receive, but everything in the world tells us the opposite. The world says that if you're going to have any money, you must hang on to it fiercely! But Jesus tells us that the way to abundance is through generosity. Interestingly enough, I've seen this principle time and again. Often the people who have the most money are the most generous. On the flip side, I've seen incredibly stingy people who are also very poor. I've seen generous people who may not have much to give, but this doesn't stop them from being generous—and even in their giving, they haven't lacked because in giving they have received. May our wealth be measured not in the abundance of our material goods, but in the fewness of our wants!

Measure 4—You Find Your Life by Losing It

In Matthew 10:39, Jesus told us, "whoever loses his life for my sake will find it." I read a book about a new trend for missionaries. Rather than living in comfortable surroundings, some missionaries today are making the decision to live with the people to whom they're ministering—specifically among the poor. One of these young missionaries told how he had left a very lavish lifestyle in the United States to live in a community that lived off of a trash dump in the Philippines. He explained that after several years of living in such poverty and sharing Jesus in the daily living routines of this trash dump community, removed from the affluence of the United States, he found his life to be far more fulfilled and rewarding than he had experienced living in material comfort.[7] This is a great living illustration of our fourth measure—that we find life by losing it.

Another example of this principle relates to a great violinist named Nicolo Paganini. He willed his marvelous violin to Genoa—the city of his birth—but only on condition that the instrument never be played again. It was an unfortunate condition, for it is a peculiarity of wood that as long as it is used and handled, it shows little wear. As soon as it is discarded, it begins to decay. The exquisite, mellow-toned violin has become worm-eaten in its beautiful case, valueless except as a relic. The moldering instrument is a reminder that a life withdrawn from all service to others loses its meaning.[8] As Jesus reminds us in Matthew 16:25, "Whoever wants to save his life will lose it, but whoever loses his life for me will find it."

Consider these questions. In the world turned upside down, are you giving your life away? Are you giving your life for Christ and for the people in your world who aren't connected to Jesus? Are you giving your life away to your co-workers, your neighbors, your church family, to the students in your class? If you want to keep your life, then the best way to do this is to give it away. God's ways aren't the same as ours. He has a different way of going about life—and His ways are enormously more effective than our ways.

Excuse Evasion

I'm insignificant. This is precisely the point! If this revolution were completely dependent on you, it would fail. That's why this revolution is so counter-intuitive—it's based out of your weakness, and it's dependant on God's strength. Corrie ten Boom (well-known survivor of the Holocaust and Nazi concentration camps), tells the story of Sadhu Sundar Singh, an Indian Christian who has had a timeless impact for Jesus. Corrie says,

> When I saw Sadhu Sundar Singh in Europe, he had completed a tour around the world. People asked him, "doesn't it do harm, your getting so much honor?" The Sadhu's answer was: "No. The donkey went into Jerusalem, and they put garments on the ground before him. He was not proud. He knew it was not done to honor him, but for Jesus, who was sitting on his back. When people honor me, I know it is not me, but the Lord, who does the job."[9]

Better to be an insignificant donkey giving Jesus a ride than a high-minded Pharisee disdainfully watching the parade.

Matthew 5:3-10 says:

> *Blessed are the poor in spirit, for theirs is the kingdom of heaven. Blessed are those who mourn, for they will be comforted. Blessed are the meek, for they will inherit the earth. Blessed are those who hunger and thirst for righteousness, for they will be filled.*

Blessed are the merciful, for they will be shown mercy. Blessed are the pure in heart, for they will see God. Blessed are the peacemakers, for they will be called sons of God. Blessed are those who are persecuted because of righteousness, for theirs is the kingdom of heaven.

Chapter 11

THE ACTIVATED REVOLUTION

activate—from the verb *to act*; from the Latin *actus*,
"a doing", and *actum*, "a thing done";
both from *agere*, "to do, set in motion, drive,
urge, chase, stir up"[1]

There's a danger in learning and growing without doing anything. Consider the story of Gillian, the daughter of Joe Slovo and Ruth First, who were leaders in the African National Congress against apartheid. Joe and Ruth were killed by a bomb sent in the mail by the South African police force during South Africa's apartheid era. Since apartheid ended, their daughter, Gillian, has traveled extensively across South Africa, seeking to help in her country's healing and restoration. In the process, she has come across many of the children of white South Africans who had been active in the oppression of non-whites. One woman, a journalist of similar age to Gillian, remarked to her:

> I know it must have been hard for you to be your parents' daughter. I know that there are many costs to be paid by the

child of heroes. But imagine how it feels to be me: to have to look at my parents, and to ask of them—how could you? How could you have witnessed all this and said nothing. How could you have let it happen?[2]

History is full of people who knew better but did nothing. Certainly, you will not be one of these individuals. So where do we go from here? How do we revolutionize our world? What's our next step? My prayer is that the words contained in this book have given you more than just food for thought. My prayer, and I believe it is God's will, is that what you read will ignite an obsession in you to be used by God to revolutionize your world—to turn your world upside down for Jesus.

In 2000, Malcolm Gladwell wrote a national best seller called *The Tipping Point*. The premise of the book is that little things can spark epidemic-size changes. He cited an example about Hush Puppies shoes in his introduction and explained how the Hush Puppies brand was about to close business in 1995 when out of the blue, for no apparent reason, the demand for these shoes went through the roof! A Hush Puppies "epidemic" literally rescued the company. The epidemic was started by a few people in East Village and Soho, New York, who wanted to wear shoes that no one else was wearing—voila, their selection of Hush Puppies.[3] Now my thinking is that if there can be a shoe outbreak for fashion purposes, there can certainly be a Jesus outbreak for eternal purposes. What would the necessary ingredients be for such an outbreak? Here are three ingredients that will activate your revolution.

The First Ingredient: Willing People

Are you a person willing to surrender to God's purposes in your life, to do something beyond yourself? Are you willing to let God work in you to be concerned about His cause? Confronted by His cause? Compelled? Corrupted and consumed? Are you willing to lean not on your own understanding, but to acknowledge God in all of your ways? What about your values? Our actions reflect our values. Are you willing to let God adjust your values? Is there space in your life for more than yourself, or have you become so self-absorbed that there's no space for anyone else?

Our world is full of people who live for themselves and are consequently very empty. Consider Kurt Cobain, the lead singer for *Nirvana*. In the days leading up to his suicide, one of his diary entries read: "Somebody, anybody, God help, help me please. I want to be accepted...I'm so tired of crying and dreaming, I'm soo soo alone."[4] Kurt lived a short, full, and tragic life. His success was astounding, and yet in the end, it wasn't enough.

God wants to help you live a life of "enough," and He is looking for people who will surrender to Him and live for something bigger and more eternal than themselves. There are enough Bill Gates, Ray Krocs, Walt Disneys, Kathrine Switzers, and Edmund Hillarys. We will always have high achievers in this world, and world records will always be broken. What has been accomplished will be accomplished again. The cycles of human victory and defeat will continue. Humanity will go on, ad nauseum, without some divine intervention. Ecclesiastes 1:9-10 says it best:

What has been will be again, what has been done will be done again; there is nothing new under the sun. Is there anything of which one can say, "Look! This is something new"? It was here already, long ago; it was here before our time.

But here's a chance to do something different, to be the individual that God made you to be. What God is looking for is people who will bow to His will, surrender to His desires, yield to His purposes, and live their lives in pursuit of pleasing Him. God isn't looking for talent—He can give you that. He isn't looking for time—He made it. He doesn't need your money since He gave it to you—think about Psalm 50:10-12:

...for every animal of the forest is mine, and the cattle on a thousand hills. I know every bird in the mountains, and the creatures of the field are mine. If I were hungry I would not tell you, for the world is mine, and all that is in it.

What God asks from you is your surrender—your willingness to let His will be more important in your life than your will. He wants you to be like Jesus, who said at Gethsemane, "yet not my will, but yours be done" (Luke 22:42). Better than Uncle Sam, God is looking for a few good men and a few good women who will allow Him to ignite a revolution in and through their lives. Christianity was never designed by God to foster selfish living. Jesus came to give His life away, and He requires us to do the same.

The Second Ingredient: An Essential Message

We have a message worth dying for, and it is truly a revolutionary message. Our cause is better than shoes or coffee. So what is our message? What did Jesus die on the Cross for? What does He want to communicate to us with His death, burial, and resurrection? Jesus died and rose from the dead first and foremost to tell us that He loves us, that He wants to have a deep and vibrant relationship with us, and that He wants to use us to bring His love, with its transformational power, to our world. This message, when conveyed and displayed in sincere and heartfelt truth on a consistent basis, changes us, as the carriers, and changes the people we bring this message to. The message is simply *Jesus is alive, He is changing our lives, and He died to connect the world to God's love.*

As a refresher, go back and read Chapter 8, when I talked about the values for this revolution—the values that are the essential message that we carry. Simply put, the revolutionary life occurs when we love the Lord our God with all of our heart, mind, and strength, as well as loving our neighbor as ourselves.

I remember when I was about 10 years old and I was thinking about my faith and what would be a good motivation to keep my faith in Jesus. Growing up in the church, I had had a few Sunday school teachers who had good intentions, but who used guilt and fear to motivate. I knew even when I was 10 that guilt and fear didn't provide much longevity for me in the motivation department. I began to think and reflect about what would be the best motive to keep me engaged in my faith in Jesus, and I came to the conclusion that love would be the most powerful force. If I could thoroughly and honestly love Jesus, then I felt that my faith would have longevity. So I found this great verse that I've prayed throughout the years and even pray daily now as an adult for my family and me—Deuteronomy 30:6: "The Lord your God will circumcise your hearts and the hearts of your descendants, so that you may love Him with all your heart and with all your soul, and live." This verse has also helped me as I love people because I know that I can't love God without loving people (see 1 John 4:8).

The Third Ingredient: Environmental Relevance

Are we willing to be carriers of Jesus, to be Jesus with skin in our world? Let's not be so religiously minded that we are no earthly good. Jesus clearly communicated that we must live with our feet on the ground, aware of and interactive with what's happening around us. We cannot merely pay lip service to this revolution—we must be active participants. Think about James 2:18, "But someone will say, 'You have faith; I have deeds.' Show me your faith without deeds, and I will show you my faith by what I do." We must bring Jesus, His love, power, and truth, to the communities that we have access to. We must not be Christian in name only. We must be Christians in action: "If anyone has material possessions and sees his brother in need but has no pity on him, how can the love of God be in him? Dear children, let us not love with words or tongue but with actions and in truth" (1 John 3:17-18).

When we look at these three ingredients, the people, the message, and the environment, we see that all of us have two of the three needed ingredients. The remaining ingredient is a question that is left up to you. Are you willing to let God use you? If you say yes, then hang on for the ride of your life! If you say no or wait, I pray that your life becomes unsettling and that your unrest will translate into relief through surrender to God.

C.S. Lewis wrote:

Imagine yourself as a living house. God comes in to rebuild that house. At first, perhaps, you can understand what he is doing. He is getting the drains right and stopping the leaks in the roof and so on. You knew that those jobs needed doing and so you are not surprised.

But presently he starts knocking the house about in a way that hurts abominably and does not seem to make sense. What on earth is he up to? The explanation is that he is building quite a different house from the one you thought of—throwing out a new wing here, putting on an extra floor there, running up towers, making courtyards.

You thought you were going to be made into a decent little cottage, but he is building a palace. He intends to come and live in it himself.[5]

Excuse Evasion

Being a revolutionary is too messy, or *it asks too much of me.* Both of these statements are true. Being a revolutionary is messy—you make mistakes; you see your humanity in painfully clear ways that you've probably avoided in the past; you're required to make changes to your life rather than making Jesus conform to you. Yes, revolution is messy. It also asks a lot of you—in fact, Jesus asks you to give Him your life. In exchange, all storms in the sky clear away; the roses begin to bloom; soft music accompanies each footstep you take; and showers of blessings suddenly overwhelm you. OK, not really. Revolution is expensive, and it will cost you a great price—mostly yourself.

Consider a few of Paul's words: "I have been crucified with Christ and I no longer live, but Christ lives in me. The life I live in the body, I live by faith in the Son of God, who loved me and gave himself for me" (Gal. 2:20). "I die every day—I mean that, brothers..." (1 Cor. 15:31). Living for the cause of Christ is a noble and worthwhile life and death—worthy of all of us.

Chapter 12

SUSTAINING THE REVOLUTION

What C.S. Lewis described, in the quote in the previous chapter, is the sustained revolution. We become the house that God rebuilds for His habitation. Having the ingredients for a Jesus revolution is thoroughly essential. But once we have these ingredients and we're seeing them become active in our lives, how do we sustain this Jesus revolution? The key is in your daily living—your habits. Habits are not bad in and of themselves. It's how they're applied in our lives that determines their worth. Consider the following example:

> Philip Haille wrote of the little village of Le Chambon in France, a town whose people, unlike others in France, hid their Jews from the Nazis. Haille went there, wondering what sort of courageous, ethical heroes could risk all to do such extraordinary good. He interviewed people in the village and was overwhelmed by the ordinariness. They weren't heroes or smart, discerning people. Haille decided that the one factor that united them was their attendance, Sunday after Sunday, at their little church, where they heard the sermons of Pastor Trochme.

Over time, they became by habit people who just knew what to do and did it. When it came time for them to be courageous, the day the Nazis came to town, they quietly did what was right. One old woman, who faked a heart attack when the Nazis came to search her house, later said, "Pastor always taught us that there comes a time in every life when a person is asked to do something for Jesus. When our time came, we knew what to do."[1]

Essentials That Sustain the Revolution

To be like the people of Le Chambon, France, we must ask ourselves what habits we should cultivate to maintain and sustain the revolution within us and to continue it on the outside. I believe with all my heart that there are a few simple necessities to remaining a Jesus revolutionary, and that without these essentials, no one will maintain the long-term revolution that Jesus intends.

These few simple necessities are the habits of daily Bible reading, daily prayer, worship, and fellowship. These habits are vital to maintaining a vibrant relationship with God. These essentials give God the platform on which He can daily continue His work in us and thereby bring about His revolution in our world through us. Generally, you cannot do what has not been done to you. So what about these necessities? How do we integrate them into our daily living?

The Bible

Frankly, I think the Bible has been underrated of late. In fact, you may initially feel turned-off by reading that the Bible is essential to sustaining the revolution in you. But truthfully, I've never met an authentic, long-term follower of Jesus who did not have the Bible integrated into their daily living. Consider the following example of how the Bible can help create and sustain a revolution:

> One of the most dramatic examples of the Bible's divine ability to transform men and women involved the famous mutiny on the "Bounty." Following their rebellion against the notorious Captain Bligh, nine mutineers, along with the Tahitian men and women who accompanied them, found their way to Pitcairn Island, a tiny dot in the South Pacific only two miles long and a mile wide. Ten years later, drink and fighting had left only one man alive—John Adams. Eleven women and 23 children made up the rest of the island's population. So far, this is the familiar story made famous in the book and motion picture. But the rest of the story is even more remarkable.
>
> About this time, Adams came across the "Bounty's" Bible in the bottom of an old chest. He began to read it, and the divine power of God's Word reached into the heart of that hardened murderer on a tiny volcanic speck in the vast Pacific Ocean and changed his life forever. The peace and love that Adams found in the Bible entirely replaced the old life of quarreling, brawling, and liquor. He began to teach the children from the Bible until every person on the island had experienced the same amazing change that he had found. Today, with a population of slightly less than 100, nearly every person on Pitcairn Island is a Christian.[2]

If there was ever a person who needed a revolution, it was John Adams—and he experienced the internal revolution that Jesus has for each of us through the Bible. Consequently, the world in which he lived was changed.

For me personally, I've found that the Bible is my lifeline. My mom has always been super-revved about the Bible, and I think I've caught some of my enthusiasm from her. Frankly, I'm glad. The Bible has saved my life on more than one occasion. I started to read through my Bible every year when I was about 12. Every year since then, minus a few years when I was in college, I've read through my Bible at least once, and I'm now in my 40s. I could never recount to you the number of times that in my daily reading God has spoken to me, encouraged me, given me direction, strengthened me, and just flat-out read my mail.

When you think about the Bible, please consider a few things the Bible can do for you, if you give it a chance.

The Bible:

1. *provides absolutes.* Psalm 119:89 says, "Your word, O Lord, is eternal...." John 17:17 says, "...Your word is truth."

2. *preserves.* Psalm 119:25 says, "...Preserve my life according to Your word."

3. *gives strength.* Psalm 119:28 says, "My soul is weary with sorrow; strengthen me according to Your word."

4. *provides focus.* Psalm 119:37 says, "Turn my eyes away from worthless things; preserve my life according to Your word."

5. *is not restricted; it is unchained.* Second Timothy 2:9 says, "...But God's word is not chained."

6. *achieves God's purposes.* Isaiah 55:11 says, "So is my word that goes out from my mouth: It will not return to me empty, but will accomplish what I desire and achieve the purpose for which I sent it." Jeremiah 1:12 says, "...for I [the Lord] am watching to see that my word is fulfilled." Lamentations 2:17 says, "The Lord has done what he planned; he has fulfilled His word...."

7. *provides direction.* Psalm 119:133 says, "Direct my footsteps according to your word; let no sin rule over me." Psalm 119:105 says, "Your word is a lamp to my feet and a light for my path."

8. *brings healing.* Psalm 107:20 says, "He sent forth his word and healed them; he rescued them from the grave."

Could I be so bold as to propose that the benefits of being in your Bible every day outweigh the excuses that you use to stay out of it? Smile, it's just a simple question.

Since you want to continue the revolution that Jesus has started in your heart and you sense that you need to have the Bible integrated into your life in a more daily way, let's get a plan. My husband was an electrical engineer for more than 10 years, and he has always said, "Sarah, if you fail to plan, you plan to fail." In the past, I've tried the daily Bible reading plan of "open and point"—open the Bible and point to something, believing that God will guide your fingers. While this has worked for me once or twice, it's too haphazard to fuel the Jesus revolution in my heart. Let me suggest a plan for you to consider that will help you read through your Bible in one year:

1. Monday-Saturday: Read two Old Testament chapters and one New Testament chapter (when you run out of the New Testament, substitute Psalms).

2. Sunday: Read three Old Testament chapters and one New Testament chapter.

If you follow this plan every day, you will read through your Bible in one year.

Now you may be thinking that you've tried to read through your Bible in the past but you got stuck in Leviticus or Exodus, bogged down with the descriptions of the tabernacle furniture. Maybe you never got past Genesis 10 where God lists a bunch of genealogies. How do you get past those parts that are less interesting? Let me give you some thoughts to ponder. When I read my Bible, I understand that it is God talking with me on a personal level. There are times when God is absolutely captivating, and there are times when I'm not as enthralled with Him. I have made the decision to remain faithful to Him in my daily Bible reading, regardless of what I am or am not getting out of it. God is a rewarder of those who diligently seek Him (see Heb. 11:6).

My commitment to reading my Bible is like my marriage commitment. I've been married to Reece for more than 13 years now, and we will both readily admit to you that every day in those years of marriage hasn't always been a holiday. And Reece will absolutely tell you that every meal has *not* been a banquet by any stretch of the imagination. Nevertheless, we are devoted to each other regardless of how we feel or how the other person is behaving. Faithfulness isn't based on what's happening externally. Faithfulness is an internal decision. Because I've made this decision to be faithful to God in my daily Bible reading,

I've learned some very amazing things about God and His faithfulness to me.

Consider the wisdom of 7-year-old Karen. This little girl's mother was startled to find her daughter going through a new Bible storybook and circling the word *God* wherever it appeared on the page. Resisting the urge to reprimand the child for defacing the book, the mother quietly asked, "Why are you doing that?" Karen answered matter-of-factly, "So that I will know where to find God when I need Him."[3]

Faithful daily Bible reading gives God an opportunity to speak to you and gives you a greater ability to recognize His voice, which leads us to the second essential—daily prayer.

Prayer

In the movie *Shadowlands*, C.S. Lewis says about prayer: "I pray because I can't help myself. I pray because I'm helpless. I pray because the need flows out of me all the time, waking and sleeping. It doesn't change God, it changes me."[4] Prayer is an interesting topic. There have been probably millions of books written on prayer and thousands of methods described to practice the necessity of prayer. It seems to me that we tend to gravitate toward either prayer or the Bible.

My journey with prayer hasn't always been one of ecstasy, to put it mildly. Truthfully, I struggled with the habit of daily prayer in my life up until about three years ago. The Bible was always very easy and engaging for me. Prayer, on the other hand, was a different story. I always knew it was important to pray, but I found it hard to practice. Do I just sit and ask God for a bunch of things? And if so, why? Doesn't He already know what I need? And what about Jesus teaching His disciples the Lord's Prayer? Should I just say this by rote every day?

I tried a few different plans that some friends had told me would really help. But I just didn't connect with any of them. So how do I pray, and what am I trying to achieve through praying? I believe that we should pray to accomplish three things, in descending order of importance.

Ask

We should *ask* God to move according to His will. Jesus tells us in John 15:7-8, "If you remain in me and my words remain in you, ask whatever you wish, and it will be given you. This is to my Father's glory, that you bear much fruit, showing yourselves to be my disciples." Asking according to God's will is essential because there can be no revolution in our world or, more importantly, in our hearts without God's will. I've tried and failed miserably to do things that weren't really integrated with or instigated by God's will. From personal experience, I can tell you that there is nothing more exhausting than trying to accomplish something bigger than yourself that is not grounded in God's will. Humans have tremendous willpower, but it's nothing compared to the power of God's will.

A great illustration of this principle can be seen in a story from the Civil War. At that time, President Abraham Lincoln met with a group of ministers for a prayer breakfast. Lincoln was not a church-goer, but he was a man of deep, if at times unorthodox, faith. At one point, one of the ministers said, "Mr. President, let us pray that God is on our side." Lincoln's response showed far greater insight. He said, "No, gentlemen, let us pray that we are on God's side."[5]

Fundamentally, prayer is an invitation from God, giving us the opportunity to allow ourselves to be drawn into being who He wants us to be and into doing what He wants us to do. But if you're like me, your next question is probably something like, "If I'm supposed to ask God to move according to His will, how do I know what His will is?"

Seek

The next depth of prayer is found in seeking out God's will in prayer. How do you know what to ask for from God if you don't know what His will is? It is through prayer and reading the Bible that we discover God's will. In Ecclesiastes 5:2, Solomon said, "Do not be quick with your mouth, do not be hasty in your heart to utter anything before God. God is in heaven and you are on earth, so let your words be few." Prayer happens when we give God the opportunity to speak to us, as we're quiet, and invite Him to show us His ways, methods, and directions.

One time there was a young man who had lost his job, and was getting uptight about his future. He decided to go see an old preacher that he knew. As he poured out his heart to the preacher, he angrily declared "I've begged and begged God to say something to help me, preacher. Why doesn't God answer?" The old preacher, who was sitting across the room, spoke a reply so quiet the young man was unable to make it out. The young man stepped across the room. "What did you say?" he asked.

The preacher repeated himself, again in a soft tone. So the young man moved closer until he was leaning on the preacher's chair. "Sorry," he said. "I still didn't hear you." With their heads bent together, the old preacher spoke once more. "God sometimes whispers," he said, "so we will move closer to hear him."[6]

I find that it's very hard to seek for God's will in my prayer time when I'm the one doing all of the talking instead of the one doing all of the listening. God spoke something noteworthy to me in relation to the amount of talking I had been doing when I prayed. While I believe it is both biblical and important to make our requests known to God, it is of *far greater value* to make sure that I hear from God than to make sure that He hears from me. Think about this—is it really all that vital that God knows exactly what you want Him to do? Or could it be more important that you receive His directions, answers, and wisdom for the various issues and frustrations in your life? At the end of the day, it is of more immeasurable and infinite value that I hear from God than that He hears from me. A core essential of seeking for God's will is listening to and for Him. Consider the following quote from the famous missionary, E. Stanley Jones:

> Prayer is surrender—surrender to the will of God and cooperation with that will. If I throw out a boathook from the boat and catch hold of the shore and pull, do I pull the shore to me, or do I pull myself to the shore? Prayer is not pulling God to my will, but the aligning of my will to the will of God.[7]

Know

Finally, and of the most supreme importance, we should pray to *know* God. Personally, I believe that this is the ultimate goal of prayer and that it should be our ultimate goal in life. In Jeremiah 9:23-24, God says to us:

> *Let not the wise man boast of his wisdom or the strong man boast of his strength or the rich man boast of his riches, but let him who boasts boast about this: that he understands and knows me, that*

I am the Lord, who exercises kindness, justice and righteousness on earth, for in these I delight....

The fundamental reason that Jesus came to earth was so we can know God. First John 5:20 says, "We know also that the Son of God has come and has given us understanding, so that we may know him who is true...." Prayer is intended by God to be the platform through which we do not merely *ask* for things. Prayer is the platform through which we *seek* out God's will. And most importantly, prayer is a vital conduit through which we come to *know* God in our hearts and not just in our minds.

Consider the following example:

Some years ago, one of England's leading actors was asked to recite for the pleasure of his fellow guests. He consented and asked if there was anything special that his audience would like to hear. After a moment's pause, an old clergyman present said: "Could you, sir, recite to us the Twenty-third Psalm?" A strange look passed over the actor's face; he paused for a moment, and then said: "I can, and I will, upon one condition; and that is that after I have recited it, you, my friend, will do the same."

"I," said the clergyman, in surprise. "But I am not an elocutionist. However, you wish it, I will do so."

Impressively, the great actor began the psalm. His voice and his intonation were perfect. He held his audience spellbound; and as he finished, a great burst of applause broke from the guests.

Then, as it died away, the old clergyman arose and began the psalm. His voice was not remarkable; his intonation was not faultless. When he had finished, no sound of applause broke the silence, but there was not a dry eye in the room, and many heads were bowed.

Then the actor rose to his feet again. His voice shook as he laid his hand upon the shoulder of the old clergyman and said: "I reached your eyes and ears, my friends; he reached your hearts. The difference is just this: I know the Twenty-third Psalm, but he knows the Shepherd."[8]

Worship

What's worship, and how is it so necessary to revolution? Let's consider the story of Joshua right before the Israelites started the revolution of conquering the land God had promised to give them (see Josh. 5). This revolution was instigated when the Israelites conquered the first major city in the Promised Land, Jericho. Right before the Israelites began marching around Jericho, maybe even the night before they started marching, Joshua had a profound experience with God. In Joshua 5:13-15, it says:

Now when Joshua was near Jericho, he [Joshua] looked up and saw a man standing in front of him with a drawn sword in his hand. Joshua went up to him and asked, "Are you for us or for our enemies?" "Neither," he replied, "but as commander of the army of the Lord I have now come." Then Joshua fell facedown to the ground in reverence, and asked him, "What message does my Lord have for his servant?" The commander of the Lord's army replied, "Take off your sandals, for the place where you are stand-ing is holy." And Joshua did so.

The success of conquering Jericho began, in many ways, with Joshua worshiping God on an individual basis. I believe this is equally true today. Worship, simply put, is the ongoing recognition that God is the boss, that God is in control, and that we are His servants.

In and of itself, worship is revolutionary because it requires us to exalt and lift up someone other than ourselves. I believe that through worship we remind ourselves that we are not in control. We remind ourselves that the God who is orchestrating this revolution is all-powerful, all-knowing, and ever-present. Through worship, we take our eyes off of ourselves, off of our accomplishments, frustrations, failures, and successes, and give ourselves thoroughly to the understanding that our God is *the* awesome God, and that there is none to compare with Him.

Let's look at worship from a very simple but effective viewpoint. When you were in school, you might have been taught the "5 W" technique in dealing with things: who, what, where, when and why. To keep it simple, let's apply this process to worship:

1. Who is worshiped? That's easy—God. Who does the worshiping? Another easy one—us.

2. What is worship? In the most direct definition, worship means to exalt, lift up, and adore. Don't get sidetracked into thinking that worship has to do with a certain kind of music or even with music at all. I worship God when I sing; I worship God when I serve others; I worship God when I give my life away. Anything that lifts up God is worship.

3. Where do we worship? Another easy one—we can worship anywhere. Don't get stuck in the quagmire by thinking that you can only worship God in church or with a CD or in a small group. Avoid that religious pitfall.

4. When do we worship? Also easy—anytime. Again, you can be religious and say that we only worship on Sundays in church—but you're believing a lie if you fall for that one.

5. Why do we worship? Now this one gets dicey really fast. If we think that we worship because God needs it, then we're belittling who God is. If we worship to get something from God (even if its something good like His anointing, power, presence, etc.), then our motives are selfish and we fundamentally contradict what worship is. If we're going to be honest, we worship for two reasons: First, we worship God because He is worthy to be exalted and lifted high, higher than anything or anyone else in our lives. Second, we worship God because it is in our design to worship Him. It is the natural order of all creation for the lesser to exalt or lift up the greater. At minimum, the lesser will always acknowledge the greater. How much more is this true from us toward God?

If we're going to see the revolution that God wants us to live, we will need to cultivate a healthy and ongoing lifestyle of worship—of lifting up God when we're driving someplace, when we're in conversation, when we're alone at home, when we're working out, and when we study. When I get discouraged about what I see happening around me, one of the most fueling things for me is to worship God, to come back to the fundamental truth that nothing is impossible with God. When

I worship, I take my eyes off of myself, off of the situations and people around me, and I put my eyes on God, who can do anything. Worship makes the revolution about God and His ways, not about us.

Community

I believe that the final essential for the revolution that Jesus wants to continue in you and perpetuate through you is community. If you think about Jesus' life, He did some completely outrageous things! He raised the dead, changed water to wine, walked on the water, rose from the dead, and a whole lot of other things that simply leave us speechless. But when you think about His life, the very first thing He did when He started His ministry on earth was to form a community. He gathered men around Him, who were known as His disciples, and formed community with these men.

Truthfully, Jesus' ministry was solidified through the community that He established. Let's think of the community that Jesus created in the terms of mortar. Mortar has three main uses: it is used as cement for bricks, it is used with a pestle to crush things (like spices and to make salsa), and it is the essential counterpart to an explosive shell (the hollowed out tube through which the explosive shell is launched). To help us think of community as being mortar through these three pictures, let's look at each picture in more depth.

Cement for Bricks

First, mortar is used as cement for bricks. Bricks by themselves have minimal strength, but when you put mortar between them, their function is fulfilled, and they become useful to their purpose. In the same way, when Jesus created community with His disciples, they each experienced strength. Consider Thomas as an example. After Jesus rose from the dead, He appeared to His disciples, but Thomas was missing. Now we know that Thomas's nickname is "doubting Thomas." But think about this: Thomas was missing when Jesus first appeared to His disciples after He rose from the dead. Thomas wasn't in the "community" when the disciples experienced the risen Jesus. But thankfully, the disciples who did experience the resurrected Jesus helped pull Thomas through his weakness of unbelief.

Look at John 20:24-28:

Now Thomas (called Didymus), one of the Twelve, was not with the disciples when Jesus came. So the other disciples told him, "We have seen the Lord!" But he said to them, "Unless I see the nail marks in His hands and put my finger where the nails were, and put my hand into His side, I will not believe it."

A week later His disciples were in the house again, and Thomas was with them. Though the doors were locked, Jesus came and stood among them and said, "Peace be with you!" Then He said to Thomas, "Put your finger here; see My hands. Reach out your hand and put it into My side. Stop doubting and believe." Thomas said to Him, "My Lord and my God!"

Have you ever struggled in your walk with God and experienced strengthening through the encouragement that you received from being in community with other believers? Community in Christ, like mortar to a brick, can strengthen and encourage us when we are weak.

Mortar and Pestle

Let's think about the second picture—that of the mortar and pestle. You may not know much about a mortar and pestle, but simply put, it is a bowl (mortar) with a blunt object (pestle) used for the purpose of crushing, grinding, or squishing. The mortar is necessary for the pestle's purpose to be fully realized. In the same way, community in Christ can help activate your purpose. For example, consider Peter, Jesus' disciple. Before Peter met Christ, he certainly had community with his fishing buddies. Peter and his brother Andrew were fishing buddies or partners in business with James and John. All four of these men worked together in the fishing industry.

When Jesus showed up, however, He spoke to Peter and told him to follow Him so that He could make him a fisher of men. Maybe Peter knew that there was something more inside of him than his life of fishing. Maybe not. But it is extremely clear that when Peter joined Jesus' disciples, he was part of Jesus' community and the purpose for his life became significantly clearer. If you watch Peter in the Book of Acts, you'll see that he's almost always accompanied by John or other disciples of Jesus.

My point is that Peter stayed in community, and his life was completely revolutionary. Peter was used by God on the day of Pentecost to lead 3,000 people to Christ. Peter was used by God to bring the Holy Spirit to the Gentiles. Peter was used by God to confront the Jewish leaders with the truth of Jesus' real identity. In all of these things, Peter stayed intricately integrated into the community of Christ. For all practical purposes, he was one of the key leaders in this growing Christian community—and through it, the purpose of his life unfolded a day at a time.

Community for us can take a lot of different shapes—small groups, Bible studies, church services, etc. Whatever the case, we need to keep our feet planted in community in Christ or, I venture to speculate, we will never reach the full potential that God has put inside of us. I know that it's easy to have difficulties when we agree to be in community in Christ. From time to time, we probably don't like our church—the sermon, or the worship, or the pastor, or the people we sit near. Nevertheless, we need the Word given to us to help us grow. We need the corporate worship to experience God's presence in ways that we may not always encounter on an individual level. We need the people, because Church is about the Body of Christ. We need each other in order to be the wholly functional Body.

Consider Psalm 92:12-14, "The righteous will flourish like a palm tree, they will grow like a cedar of Lebanon; planted in the house of the Lord, they will flourish in the courts of our God. They will still bear fruit in old age, they will stay fresh and green." We need to be in a small group, like a Bible study or prayer group that facilitates conversations relating to the Bible and our faith and emphasizes receiving ministry and ministering to others. Small groups can become challenging because we're required to be good at forgiveness and to not isolate ourselves. Small groups require us to grow as individuals and in the way we interact with others. A great book that can help you discover the value and need for small groups is *How People Grow* by Henry Cloud and John Townsend.[9] This has been really powerful in my life and has helped me to see how mortar, or community, is essential to being a revolutionary for Jesus.

Mortar and Shell

Finally, when we think about community in Christ and the picture of mortar, let's finish by looking at a mortar and shell. While I'm not in any way a weapons expert, I understand that a shell is an explosive that can be launched through a mortar—a hollow tube. It is interesting to note that the shell travels in the direction that the mortar is pointed when the shell is launched. The same is true with community in general. Think about it—your friends influence the direction of your life, negatively or positively. By being in community in Christ, you put yourself in a position where the community can positively influence you to follow Christ and even challenge you to grow in Christ, allowing His revolution to infiltrate every area of your life! Community in Christ is essential to keeping Jesus' revolution thriving in your heart as well as in your world.

In Conclusion

Let's summarize the four things that will help you maintain and grow the revolution that Jesus has for you and your world. First, the Bible is a daily necessity to feed you and keep you moving in the right direction with Jesus. Second, prayer is the platform through which God will speak to you and direct you in His will. Third, worship positions you to acknowledge the proper alignment of your life with God—He's in charge and we live to lift Him up. Fourth and finally, community keeps us grounded in living Jesus' revolution through our relationships, and it also encourages us to live as an extravagant revolutionary for Jesus.

As we finish our time together, let's consider that we started with Paul as our example of leading a Jesus revolution. One of the primary objectives that Paul lived for was to know Christ:

What is more, I consider everything a loss compared to the sur-passing greatness of knowing Christ Jesus my Lord, for whose sake I have lost all things. I consider them rubbish, that I may gain Christ and be found in him, not having a righteousness of my own that comes from the law, but that which is through faith in Christ—the righteousness that comes from God and is by faith. I want to know Christ and the power of his resurrection and the fellowship of sharing in his sufferings, becoming like him in his death, and so, somehow, to attain to the resurrection from the dead (Philippians 3:8-11).

There is not a person on this earth that will not be revolutionized by knowing Jesus. And there's not a person on this earth who will not revolutionize their world if they know Jesus.

The ingredients that we need for the revolution Jesus has are will-ing people, Jesus' essential message, and environmental relevance. How we sustain this revolution inside us as individuals is through our daily habits of prayer, Bible reading, worship, and community in Christ. Let me leave you with a parting idea or even a small place to begin. Something I've found to be really helpful and revolutionary for me in both small and massive ways is to pray certain Bible verses every day. Here are a few that I pray; maybe you could consider praying one, some, or all of these daily as well:

I keep asking that the God of our Lord Jesus Christ, the glorious Father, may give you the Spirit of wisdom and revelation, so that you may know him better. I pray also that the eyes of your heart may be enlightened in order that you may know the hope to which he has called you, the riches of his glorious inheritance in the saints, and his incomparably great power for us who believe... (Ephesians 1:17-19).

I will give them a heart to know me, that I am the Lord... (Jeremiah 24:7).

The Lord your God will circumcise your hearts and the hearts of your descendants, so that you may love him with all your heart and with all your soul, and live (Deuteronomy 30:6).

...We have not stopped praying for you and asking God to fill you with the knowledge of his will through all spiritual wisdom and understanding. And we pray this in order that you may live a life worthy of the Lord and may please him in every way: bearing fruit in every good work, growing in the knowledge of God, being strengthened with all power according to his glorious might so that you may have great endurance and patience, and joyfully giving thanks to the Father... (Colossians 1:9-12).

I will give them singleness of heart and action, so that they will always fear me for their own good and the good of their children after them (Jeremiah 32:39).

My sheep listen to my voice; I know them, and they follow me (John 10:27).

Be the revolution you want to see. Refuse to live a life of complaints, gripes, regrets, materialism, selfish ambition, and mediocrity. Let Jesus perpetuate His revolution in your life, to revolutionize your world.

ENDNOTES

Chapter 1—Revolution in Person

1. "About McDonald's," *McDonald's Corporation*, http://www.mcdonalds.com/corp/about.html (accessed 26 April 2005).

2. http://en.wikipedia.org/wiki/Walt_Disney (accessed 26 April 2005).

3. http://en.wikipedia.org/wiki/Bill_Gates (accessed 26 April 2005).

4. Cover photo, *Time Magazine* vol. 133, #25 (June 19, 1989).

5. Mother Teresa, http://scholar.lib.vt.edu/VA-news/VA-Pilot/issues/1997/vp970914/09140190.htm (accessed 26 April 2005).

6. http://www.essortment.com/all/motherteresahi_rmgp.htm (accessed 26 April 2005).

7. http://en.wikipedia.org/wiki/Mother_Teresa (accessed 26 April 2005).

8. http://en.wikipedia.org/wiki/Tom_Dempsey (accessed 26 April 2005).

9. http://www.quoteworld.org/quotes/6579 (accessed 26 April 2005).

10. *Wikipedia*, s.v. "Mount Everest," http://en.wikipedia.org/wiki/Mount_Everest (accessed 26 April 2005).

11. Peter Gambaccini, "Unforgettable: The 40 Most Influential People and Moments of the Past Four Decades," *Runner's World* (13 Oct. 2006), http://www.runnersworld.com/article/0,7120,s6-243-297—10545-0,00.html (accessed 14 Feb. 2008).

12. *Ibid*.

13. Nelson Mandela, quoted in *Wikipedia*, s.v. "Nelson Maldela," http://en.wikipedia.org/wiki/Nelson_Mandela (accessed 14 Oct. 2007).

Chapter 2—Revolution in the Bible

1. http://www.bibleplaces.com/thessalonica.htm (accessed 12 March 2008).

2. Craig S. Keener, *The IVP Bible Background Commentary: New Testament* (Downers Grove, IL: InterVarsity Press, 1994), 362.

3. *International Standard Bible Encyclopedia*, Electronic Database, (Seattle, WA: Biblesoft, Inc., 2003).

4. Personal research covering several years.

5. Petronius, quoted in *Adam Clarke's Commentary*, electronic database (Seattle, WA: Biblesoft, Inc, 2003).

6. "The Growth of Early Christianity," *Christian History* 57 (1998), 26.

7. *Wikipedia*, s.v. "Bill & Melinda Gates Foundation," http://en.wikipedia.org/wiki/Gates_foundation#_note-10 (accessed 26 April 2005).

8. John F. Kennedy, quoted by *The Quotations and Sayings* Database, http://www.quotesandsayings.com (accessed 15 Oct. 2007).

9. Fidel Castro, quoted by *The Quotations and Sayings Database*, http://www.quotesandsayings.com (accessed 15 Oct. 2007).

10. Ernesto Che Guevara, quoted by *The Quotations Page*, http://www.quotationspage.com (accessed.15 Oct. 2007).

11. Eric Hoffer, quoted in *The Quotations and Sayings Database*, http://www.quotesandsayings.com (accessed 15 Oct. 2007).

12. All quotes from "Famous False Predictions," *Oz Sermon Illustrations*, http://www.ozsermonillustrations.com/frames/ knowledge,_truth_frameset.htm (accessed 15 Oct. 2007).

Chapter 3—Revolution for Beginners

1. http://dictionary.reference.com/browse/ignite (accessed 14 Oct. 2007).

2. Polycarp, quoted in "The Stories Behind Famous Christian Quotes, *Christian History Institute*, http://chi.gospelcom.net/ quotes/quote005.shtml (accessed 14 Oct. 2007).

3. Deitrich Bonhoeffer, quoted in Geffrey B. Kelly, "The Life and Death of a Modern Martyr," *Christian History*, 32 (1991), 15-16.

4. *Ibid.*, 33.

5. George Bernard Shaw, "Maxims for Revolutionists," *Man and Superman*, quoted in *The Quotations Page*, http://www.quotationspage.com (accessed 14 Oct. 2007).

6. Anthony J. D'Angelo, *The College Blue Book: A Few Thoughts, Reflections & Reminders on How to Get the Most Out of College & Life* (Arkad Press, 1995), quoted in The Quotations Page, http://www.quotationspage.com (accessed 14 Oct. 2007).

7. William Byron Forbush, ed., *Fox's Book of Martyrs: A History of the Lives, Sufferings and Deaths of the Early Christian and Protestant Martyrs* (Grand Rapids, MI: Zondervan, 1987).

8. Tertullian, quoted by *The Quotations and Sayings Database*, http://www.quotesandsayings.com (accessed 14 Oct. 2007).

Chapter 4—Lesson 1

1. *The Online Etymology Dictionary*, s.v. "concern," http://www.etymonline.com (accessed 15 Oct. 2007).

2. *The Online Etymology Dictionary*, s.v. "confront," http://www.etymonline.com (accessed 15 Oct. 2007).

3. Information from personal class notes.

4. http://www.factcheck.org/article133.html (accessed 15 Oct 2007).

5. http://www.umich.edu/news/Releases/2004/Dec04/04drugpr_complete.pdf; 10 (accessed 14 Oct. 2007). Survey by University of Michigan News and Information Services, 21 Dec. 2004.

6. Lloyd D. Johnston, et al., *Monitoring the Future: National Survey Results on Drug Use*, 1975-2003: Volume II, College Students and Adults Ages 19-45, (Bethesda, MD: National Institute on Drug Abuse, 2004), 35; http://monitoringthefuture.org/pubs/monographs/vol2_2003.pdf (accessed 14 Oct. 2007).

7. U.S. Department of Justice, "Indicators of School Crime and Safety, 2004," *Bureau of Justice Statistics*, http://www.ojp.usdoj.gov/bjs/abstract/iscs04.htm (accessed 14 Oct. 2007).

8. *Divorce Statistics*, http://www.divorcestatistics.org (accessed 14 Oct. 2007).

9. Beverly Bliss, "Step Families," *Parenthood in America*, http://parenthood.library.wisc.edu/Bliss/Bliss.html (accessed 14 Oct. 2007).

10. http://www.kff.org/youthhivstds/upload/U-S-Teen-Sexual-Activity-Fact-Sheet.pdf, p. 1 (accessed 14 Oct. 2007).

11. Eric Tiansay, "Running From God," *Charisma Magazine* (Sept. 2005), http://www.charismamag.com/display.php?id=11707 (accessed 14 Oct. 2007).

12. http://www.allbusiness.com/population-demograph-ics/demographic-groups-generation-x/6256035-1.html (accessed 14 Oct. 2007).

13. Switchfoot, "Meant to Live," *The Beautiful Letdown* (Columbia Records, 2003).

14. "Playing it Safe," *Oz Sermon Illustrations*, adapted from Illustrations Unlimited, http://www.ozsermonillustrations.com/frames/fear_frameset.htm (accessed 14 Oct. 2007).

Chapter 5—Lesson 2

1. *The Online Etymology Dictionary*, s.v. "compelled," http://www.etymonline.com (accessed 14 Oct. 2007).

2. *The Online Etymology Dictionary*, s.v. "corrupted," http://www.etymonline.com (accessed 14 Oct. 2007).

3. "Industrial Revolution," *The Columbia Encyclopedia, Sixth Edition* (Columbia University Press, 2007), on *Bartleby.com*, http://www.bartleby.com/65/in/IndustR.html (accessed 14 Oct. 2007).

4. "A Son to a Dying Man," *Oz Sermon Illustrations*, http://www.ozsermonillustraions.com/frames/kindness_frame set.htm (accessed 14 Oct. 2007).

5. "The Busy Samaritan," *Oz Sermon Illustrations*,
    http://www.ozsermonillustrations.com/frames/time_frameset.h
    tm (accessed 14 Oct. 2007).

6. Eleanor H. Porter, quoted in *The Quotations Page*,
    http://www.quotationspage.com (accessed 14 Oct. 2007).

Chapter 6—Lesson 3

1. *The Online Etymology Dictionary*, s.v. "consume,"
    http://www.etymonline.com (accessed 14 Oct. 2007).

2. *Wikipedia*, s.v. "Vladimir Lenin," http://en.wikipedia.org
    (accessed 15 Oct. 2007).

3. Read Robert Conquest's "Harvest of Sorrow" (Oxford
    University Press, 1986) for a thorough discussion of this topic.

4. http://en.wikipedia.org/wiki/Stalin#Number_of_victims
    (accessed 15 Oct. 2007).

5. http://chi.gospelcom.net/GLIMPSEF/Glimpses/
    glmps047.shtml (accessed 15 Oct. 2007).

6. http://www.wholesomewords.org/missions/biotaylor7.html
    (accessed 12 March 2008).

7. Heard as part of a sermon.

8. http://net.bible.org/illustration.php?topic=862 (accessed 15
    Oct. 2007).

9. Martin Luther King Jr., quoted in *The Quotations and Sayings
    Database*, http://www.quotesandsayings.com (accessed 15 Oct.
    2007).

Chapter 7—Reality Meets Revolution

1. *The Online Etymology Dictionary*, s.v. "application," http://www.etymonline.com (accessed 15 Oct. 2007).

2. Information from personal class notes.

3. John Piper, "George Muller's Strategy for Showing God," Desiring God: Resource Library (2004), http://www.desiringgod.org (accessed 15 Oct. 2007). *Wikipedia*, s.v. "George Muller," http://en.wikipedia.org (accessed 15 Oct. 2007).

4. For a more thorough discussion on Bono's life and humanitarian efforts, see "Bono in Conversation with Michka Assayas" (Penguin Group, 2006).

5. Heard on one of Joel Osteen's television programs in 2007.

6. http://en.wikipedia.org/wiki/John_Bradford (accessed 15 Oct. 2007).

Chapter 8—Revolution Essentials

1. *The Online Etymology Dictionary*, s.v. "value," http://www.etymonline.com (accessed 15 Oct. 2007).

2. For the complete story of Starbucks and its history with Howard Schultz, see Howard Schultz and Dori Jones Yang, *Pour Your Heart Into It: How Starbucks Built a Company One Cup at a Time* (New York, NY: Hyperion Books, 1999).

3. "The Menninger Clinic," *Oz Sermon Illustrations*, http://www.ozsermonillustrations.com/frames/love_frameset.htm (accessed 15 Oct. 2007).

4. "Loving Your Enemies (Martin Luther King Jr. Quote)," *Oz Sermon Illustrations*, http://www.ozsermonillustrations.com/frames/love_frameset.htm (accessed 15 Oct. 2007).

5.   Bill Hybels, *Who You Are When No One's Looking: Choosing Consistency, Resisting Compromise* (Downers Grove, IL: InterVarsity Press, 1987), 35.

6.   http://www.nndb.com/people/977/000024905/ (accessed 12 March 2008).

7.   Bits & Pieces (May 1990) 10, quoted in *Oz Sermon Illustrations*, http://www.sermonillustrations.com/a-z/c/children.htm (accessed 15 Oct. 2007).

8.   Nicolas Copernicus, quoted in *The Quotations and Sayings Database*, http://www.quotesandsayings.com (accessed 15 Oct. 2007).

Chapter 9—Revolution in Values and Vision

1.   *The Online Etymology Dictionary*, s.v. "backward," http://www.etymonline.com (accessed15 Oct 2007).

2.   http://www.makeitclearnow.org/relhumor.html (accessed 15 Oct. 2007).

3.   http://www.usa-patriotism.com/heroes/first_patriots.htm (accessed 15 Oct. 2007).

4.   http://dictionary.reference.com/browse/acknowledge (accessed 15 Oct. 2007).

5.   Sonia Johnson, quoted in the *Quotations and Sayings Database*, http://www.quotesandsayings.com (accessed 16 Oct. 2007).

Chapter 10—The Plan for Revolution

1.   *The Online Etymology Dictionary*, s.v. "change," http://www.etymonline.com (accessed 16 Oct. 2007).

2. Andrew Murray, http://www.higherpraise.com/illustrations/
    surrender.htm (accessed 16 Oct. 2007).

3. "Humility," *Sermon Illustrations*, http://www.sermonillustra
    tions.com/a-z/h/humility.htm (accessed 16 Oct. 2007).

4. Knofel Stanton, *Heaven Bound Living* (Cincinnati, OH:
    Standard, 1989), 35.

5. *Closer Walk* (December, 1991), quoted in "Humility," Sermon
    Illustrations, http://www.sermonillustrations.com/a-z/h/humil
    ity.htm (accessed 16 Oct. 2007).

6. "Generosity," *Sermon Illustrations*, http://www.sermonillustra
    tions.com/a-z/g/generosity.htm (accessed 16 Oct. 2007).

7. For a complete description of this trend throughout the world,
    read "The New Friars: The Emerging Movement Serving the
    World's Poor" by Scott Bessenecker (IVP, 2006).

8. http://www.sermonillustrations.com/a-z/s/servant.htm
    (accessed 16 Oct. 2007)

9. Corrie Ten Boom, *Each New Day*, quoted in *Sermon
    Illustrations*, http://www.sermonillustrations.com/a-z/h/
    humility.htm (accessed 16 Oct. 2007).

Chapter 11—The Activated Revolution

1. *The Online Etymology Dictionary*, s.v. "activate,"
    http://www.etymonline.com (accessed 16 Oct. 2007).

2. Gillian Slovo, "Making history: South Africa's Truth and
    Reconciliation Commission," *Open Democracy Ltd*, (May 12,
    2002), http://www.opendemocracy.net/democracy-
    africa_democracy/article_818.jsp (accessed 16 Oct. 2007).

3. For a thorough discussion on revolutionary changes that begin
    with small things, read Malcolm Gladwell's, *The Tipping Point:*

How Little Things Can Make a Big Difference (Boston: Back Bay Books, 2000).

4. Kurt Cobain, quoted in Charles Cross, *Heavier Than Heaven: A Biography of Kurt Cobain* (New York, NY: Hyperion, 2001), quoted in "Kurt Cobain," Oz Sermon Illustrations, http://www.ozsermonillustrations.com/frames/loneliness_fram eset.htm (accessed 16 Oct. 2007).

5. C.S. Lewis, *Mere Christianity* (San Francisco: Harper, 1952), 205.

Chapter 12—Sustaining the Revolution

1. William H. Willimon, *Pulpit Digest*, quoted in "Habits," Sermon Illustrations, http://www.sermonillustrations.com/a-z/h/habits.htm (accessed 16 Oct. 2007).

2. *Signs of the Times* (Aug. 1988) 5, quoted in "Bible, Power of," *Sermon Illustrations*, http://www.sermonillustrations.com/a-z/b/bible_power_of.htm (accessed 16 Oct. 2007).

3. http://elbourne.org/sermons/index.mv?illustration+3486 (accessed 16 Oct. 2007).

4. C.S. Lewis, quoted in *Shadowlands*, VHS, directed by Richard Attenborough (Oxford, England: Price Entertainment, 1993).

5. http://www.ozsermonillustrations.com/frames/prayer_ frameset.htm (accessed 16 Oct. 2007).

6. http://www.brethren.org.nz/inspirational/ (accessed 16 Oct. 2007).

7. E. Stanley Jones, quoted in Kent Hughes and Barbara Hughes, *Liberating Ministry from the Success Syndrome* (Carol Stream, IL: Tyndale House Publishers, 1988), 73.

8. http://www.happyposts.com/profiles/blog/show?id= 665784%3ABlogPost%3A13979 (accessed 16 Oct. 2007).

9. Dr. Henry Cloud and Dr. John Townsend, *How People Grow: What the Bible Reveals About Personal Growth* (Grand Rapids, MI: Zondervan, 2001).

Keeping My Faith

Sarah Bowling
PO Box 6598
Denver, CO 80155
E-mail: SarahBowling@mhmin.org
Websites: www.world-child.org and www.mhmin.org

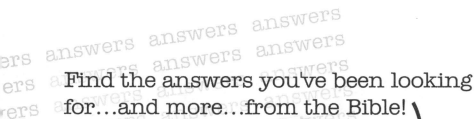

Additional copies of this book and other
book titles from DESTINY IMAGE are
available at your local bookstore.

Call toll-free: 1-800-722-6774.

Send a request for a catalog to:

Destiny Image® Publishers, Inc.

P.O. Box 310
Shippensburg, PA 17257-0310

*"Speaking to the Purposes of God for This
Generation and for the Generations to Come."*

For a complete list of our titles,
visit us at www.destinyimage.com.